Building Competitive Regions

Strategies and Governance

ORGANISATION FOR ECONOMIC CO-OPERATION AND DEVELOPMENT

ORGANISATION FOR ECONOMIC CO-OPERATION AND DEVELOPMENT

The OECD is a unique forum where the governments of 30 democracies work together to address the economic, social and environmental challenges of globalisation. The OECD is also at the forefront of efforts to understand and to help governments respond to new developments and concerns, such as corporate governance, the information economy and the challenges of an ageing population. The Organisation provides a setting where governments can compare policy experiences, seek answers to common problems, identify good practice and work to co-ordinate domestic and international policies.

The OECD member countries are: Australia, Austria, Belgium, Canada, the Czech Republic, Denmark, Finland, France, Germany, Greece, Hungary, Iceland, Ireland, Italy, Japan, Korea, Luxembourg, Mexico, the Netherlands, New Zealand, Norway, Poland, Portugal, the Slovak Republic, Spain, Sweden, Switzerland, Turkey, the United Kingdom and the United States. The Commission of the European Communities takes part in the work of the OECD.

OECD Publishing disseminates widely the results of the Organisation's statistics gathering and research on economic, social and environmental issues, as well as the conventions, guidelines and standards agreed by its members.

This work is published on the responsibility of the Secretary-General of the OECD. The opinions expressed and arguments employed herein do not necessarily reflect the official views of the Organisation or of the governments of its member countries.

Publié en français sous le titre :
Promouvoir la compétitivité des régions
Stratégies et gouvernance

© OECD 2005

No reproduction, copy, transmission or translation of this publication may be made without written permission. Applications should be sent to OECD Publishing: *rights@oecd.org* or by fax (33 1) 45 24 13 91. Permission to photocopy a portion of this work should be addressed to the Centre français d'exploitation du droit de copie, 20, rue des Grands-Augustins, 75006 Paris, France (*contact@cfcopies.com*).

Foreword

This report analyses the strategies pursued by member governments to address the competitiveness of regional economies and the accompanying governance mechanisms on which the implementation of these strategies rests. The report is principally based on findings from the series of reviews undertaken by OECD at national and regional level.

Beginning with an overview of the concept of competitiveness, the first chapter looks at how this term has been employed recently in a regional context and how it is being translated into policy. Chapter 1 concludes that there are two broad categories of policy, those relating to firms and those relating to the wider business environment. Chapter 2 assesses the main instruments that have been used to increase the productivity of firms, focusing on three types of policy oriented mainly to increase the level of innovation: science parks and other land-based initiatives, cluster policies and policies to link local research institutions with enterprise. Chapter 3 turns to the enabling environment in which firms operate, identifying the main factors that increase the attractiveness of a region as a residential and business location. The overall conclusion of Part I of this report is that regional competitiveness policies, by their nature, are making new demands on both central and local governments in terms of policy formulation and implementation. As such, the evolutions that are apparent in the systems of governance in member countries are increasingly crucial.

Assessment of these evolutions in the second part of this report demonstrates that these multi-level governance mechanisms are moving towards more co-operative practices. First, the vertical relations between the centre and sub-national governments are examined, with particular reference to the advantages and disadvantages of the use of contractual arrangements between levels of government (Chapter 4). Among other things, co-ordination between sectors/departments at the level of the central government stands out as an important pre-requisite for more effective delivery of policy at lower levels. The report then looks at horizontal co-ordination at local and regional level, in particular co-ordination between municipalities and the different local institutional structures that can promote such co-operation (Chapter 5). Extending the analysis of cross-jurisdictional co-operation, the report then addresses the increasingly important case of cross-border governance structures. Finally, the role of new actors, both private firms and civil society organisations, in multi-level governance is examined, clarifying the role that the centre can play in facilitating such public-private partnerships (Chapter 6). Concluding our discussion of governance issues, the last chapter addresses three main issues common to the various devices that have been reviewed (Chapter 7).

Acknowledgements. *This report was prepared by Claire Charbit and Andrew Davies, with the assistance of Adrienne Hervé. In addition to input from OECD territorial reviews, the report also draws on material prepared for the OECD by John Bachtler, Director of the European Policies Research Centre (EPRC), and contributions to an OECD Symposium on Multi-Level Governance held in June 2003 by Luigi Bobbio, Professor, Università di Torino, Italy, Jean-Pierre Collin, Professor, Université du Québec à Montréal (UQAM), Gerard Marcou, Professor, Université de Paris (Pantheon-Sorbonne), France and Paul Vermeylen, Expert Consultant, Brussels, Belgium.*

Table of Contents

Executive Summary.. 7

Part I. **Strategies** 19

    1. Competitiveness in a regional context 20
    2. Competitive firms: policies to generate innovation and knowledge .. 26
    3. Competitive regions: policies for the wider business environment . 50
    Notes 63

Part II. **Governance** 67

    4. Coordination between the different levels of government: transfers, contracting practices and incentives.......................... 69
    5. Horizontal co-ordination 91
    6. New actors in economic development strategies 114
    7. Common issues in co-operative governance 124
    Notes 130

Bibliography 135

List of boxes

    1.1. Targeted regulatory reform initiatives: Japan's Special Zones...... 23
    1.2. Region type and competitiveness strategy: some examples 25
    1.3. Sophia-Antipolis: slow evolution 31
    1.4. Cluster development: a national approach and a regional model in Japan 35
    1.5. Cluster audit in Montreal... 36
    1.6. Cluster policies: success involves intensive effort: the case of Scotland 37
    1.7. Research-industry relationships: the example of Georgia Tech 43
    1.8. Higher education and industrial clusters in the Öresund region.... 44
    1.9. Deregulation of universities: the case of Japan 46
    1.10. Centres of Expertise, Finland.................................... 48
    1.11. HES in Switzerland 50
    1.12. Impacts of the Öresund bridge on attractiveness and competitiveness... 54
    1.13. Some examples of rural amenities assessed by OECD 56
    1.14. Reorientation of industrial cities: the port city of Busan, Korea 61
    1.15. The balance sheet of urban amenity promotion in Glasgow 62

2.1. Metropolitan reform: the creation of the Greater London Authority   94
2.2. Illustrations of reticence with regard to inter-municipal mergers   97
2.3. The US case   98
2.4. An illustration of place-based policy in rural areas: the micro-regions   100
2.5. Inter-municipal co-operation in intermediate regions   103
2.6. Examples of intermediate levels for co-ordinating inter-municipality agreements   107
2.7. Cross-border governance: the examples of TriRhena and Öresund   111
2.8. Obstacles to cross border institution building: the starting point for Vienna-Bratislava   112
2.9. The example of Cascadia   113
2.10. PPPs for local innovation   116
2.11. PPPs for the supply of local infrastructure   117
2.12. Participatory PPPs for "territorial projects"   118
2.13. Logistic Centre Wolfsburg GmbH – Germany   121
2.14. Expertise advice and comprehension between public and private sectors – The Netherlands   123
2.15. Examples of learning initiatives for local public officials in OECD countries   127

List of tables

1.1. Taxonomy of kinds of relationships between tertiary education and business   41
1.2. Source of innovative ideas for Busan firms   46
1.3. Types of collective action for mise en valeur of amenities   59
1.4. Port city transition   61

List of figures

1.1. Transport infrastructure investment and economic growth effects   52
2.1. Indicators of fiscal decentralisation in OECD countries: sub-national government share in general government revenues and expenditures, percentages, 2002   71
2.2. Changes in the share of sub-national governments in total public revenues and spending   71
2.3. Shares of conditional transfers   72
2.4. Organisational structure for regional contracts   76

ISBN 92-64-00946-9
Building Competitive Regions
Strategies and Governance
© OECD 2005

Executive Summary

EXECUTIVE SUMMARY

The challenge for territorial policymakers is to develop policies that are effective and relevant in different regional contexts

In recent years, the main focus of territorial policy has been on sustaining growth, not only on addressing relative decline but on making regions more competitive. This has involved a shift away from redistribution and subsidies for lagging regions in favour of measures to increase the productivity of enterprises and encourage private investment, including an emphasis on endogenous assets.

Putting this into practice is, however, complicated because different regions have different characteristics (urban, intermediate, industrial, rural, etc.) which in turn imply specific and different policy and investment needs. As a first principle, therefore, policies to improve competitiveness need to be capable of adapting to these different needs.

In all cases, competitiveness policies represent a governance challenge

Regional competitiveness policies also pose significant governance challenges. On the one hand, they depend on effective integration of sectoral policies such as R&D and education. They also demand close co-operation across levels of government and between neighbouring regions, not to mention resource-sharing. They also involve a high degree of co-ordination in planning and spatial development (zoning, network infrastructure development, etc.). As important as the choice of strategy is the framework within which the strategy is implemented.

Policies for firms focus increasingly on measures that promote innovation
… But the instruments appear to favour more advanced regions

Knowledge-based strategies stand out as key elements of new regional policy, and they exemplify the move towards building on existing, endogenous assets. National and regional governments are re-orienting their policies to emphasise the role of public policy in creating or facilitating more systematic exchange and interaction among key economic actors. This orientation is driven by recognition that the system by which knowledge is created and then circulates is an important determinant of productivity in a regional context. This report assesses three of the most common categories of policy measures that endeavour to build such interlinkages:

1. **Real estate based projects**: development of science parks, technopoles and other industrial spaces designed to facilitate networking and technology development and transfer through "co-location".
2. **Cluster-type policies**: initiatives to support existing or nascent groupings of firms by providing collective services and other measures to build co-operation within the cluster and to enable joint initiatives to export, market, etc.
3. **Linking research and industry**: linking knowledge producers with users in order to promote "systems" of technology and innovation diffusion and better commercialisation of innovation.

Among the three instruments discussed in this report, each has significant advantages and some disadvantages, and there is some complementarity. It is apparent that in the search for regional policies that emphasise knowledge and innovation, these approaches are appealing, individually and in combination.

For other regions, instruments need to be adapted, but this risks diluting their impact…

However, the emphasis on innovation and knowledge has some limitations. In particular, it appears to rest on an assumption that regions have at least moderate levels of "knowledge infrastructure" and that local enterprises have some innovative capacity. The three instruments discussed in the report all appear to be best suited to more advanced regions. In order to be cost-effective and have regional impact in other types of regions, these policies need to be significantly adapted in less amenable contexts than are found in the "best practice" high-tech, high wage regions. So far, adapting innovation-led policies appears often to dilute their impact. For example, the development of ambitious technology parks in less advanced regions has generally been seen to produce very limited results – the term "cathedrals in the desert" has been used to describe them. Cluster policies appear to depend on the presence of factors that are by no means universal in intermediate and rural regions (*e.g.*, sectoral specialisations, networking culture, etc.). A stronger participation by technical colleges in regional development is an important avenue for policymakers; however, it is dependent on the quality of the educational institution concerned and the flexibility of its mission. Other measures to embed FDI and to foster entrepreneurship have also had mixed results outside the main economic centres.

Policies should focus on the enabling environment as a factor that promotes business activity

The common denominator in current thinking about territorial policy – including in relation to knowledge and innovation – is an emphasis on exploiting place-specific externalities and unused potential. Policy instruments now tend to focus on providing collective goods that improve what has been termed the "enabling environment" or the "quality of place" – the attractiveness and functioning of the region as a whole. These were often formerly part of social or environmental policies, but are now increasingly framed in terms of building competitiveness.

Investment in the enabling environment emphasises physical infrastructure investment, but the constraints on infrastructure investment are growing. In particular, the costs of new infrastructure have increased dramatically, while the proportion of total investment that will need to be allocated to maintenance is becoming more significant. As a result, policymakers are seeking more cost-effective strategies.

In theory, investment in the regional environment should aim to trigger positive externalities that already exist in the region, which in turn should produce growth effects via more intense and productive economic activity. The issue for policymakers is to identify the possible sources of externalities in regions where economic activity is, for one reason or another, constrained (for example because of remoteness, because of location in a deprived urban area, or because of the presence of political-administrative borders).

Rural policies should emphasise the potential of ICT and of amenities in providing a base for enterprise development…

Recent moves to diversify rural economies have shifted the emphasis towards concepts of rural development that include both sectoral and non-sectoral initiatives designed to maintain traditional sectors whilst supporting the emergence of new activities. The concept of competitiveness applied to rural regions is still relatively new, but it is having an important influence on policymaking. Adoption of this more positive approach to rural policy has

increased interest in more market-oriented solutions to the problems of rural regions. Two domains appear particularly important:
- *Communications infrastructure* produces generalisable time-savings and productivity gains for most economic sectors. There is a close link between the increased use of ICT in rural locations and growing interest among policymakers in rural enterprise creation, including how cluster policies can be adapted to be relevant for rural regions.
- *Amenities* can provide the basis for a wide range of economic activities in rural regions, particularly tourism-related activities but also other industries that support SMEs and provide a focus for entrepreneurship.

While urban regions are generally receptive to innovation-led policies, governments are still confronted with localised problems of adjustment…

In general, policies to improve the competitiveness of cities emphasise their comparative advantages in terms of knowledge infrastructure and the range and variety of interactions among diverse economic actors. As noted above, innovation-led policies of the type discussed in this report are generally applicable in urban regions, and the main success stories related to these approaches tend to be found in and around metropolitan areas (though not exclusively so).

… In such cases, an urban "amenity" approach can help improve the enabling environment

Nonetheless, governments continue to emphasise the challenges of restructuring industrial economies and the problems of maintaining economic and social vitality in particular areas of cities (whether inner city or suburbs). In such cases, policymakers have recognised that they need to address the quality of the wider urban environment in addition to direct initiatives for the enterprise sector. In this respect, greater use of the framework developed by OECD for rural amenities would be appropriate with respect to creation of markets for collective public goods and the tools for supporting collective action and public-private partnerships to transform urban land use patterns and regenerate deprived neighbourhoods.

EXECUTIVE SUMMARY

Cross-border regions exemplify the links between competitiveness and governance

Cross border regions represent another case in which the overall strategy to improve the competitiveness of the region generally needs to address issues relating to the enabling environment as well as promoting objectives relating to firms directly. The cross-border integration issue exemplifies the governance challenges that policymakers face in implementing development strategies that are specific enough to provide relevant solutions for a given region, but that are also coherent with national objectives.

The quality of the enabling environment is determined in large part by the quality of local collective competition goods…

The emphasis on the quality of the local environment for business leads directly to the question of the quality of locally provided services and public goods. Firms, especially SMEs, are dependent on the environment in which they are located to provide them with different types of "local collective competition goods". This involves the participation of various categories of actors – public authorities at local, regional and central levels, private firms or non profit organisations, etc. – to ensure that the provision is appropriate, relevant, high quality, and so on. For example, regional innovation systems are based on relations between industry and universities, between small and large enterprises, and between sectors (training and employment, for example). At central level, budgets, like the strategies themselves, relate to different ministerial portfolios. And, in a context of decentralisation different sectors are the competence of different levels of government. The co-ordination of the various actors and sectors implied in such "systems" can be defined as mechanisms of multi-level governance, and can be seen to directly influence competitiveness.

… Of which the high quality provision is increasingly dependent on processes of co-operation among key government and non-government actors

New forms of governance targeting local and regional competitiveness, like most development strategies themselves, are increasingly oriented towards co-operation. This is true with respect to both vertical linkages (between lower and higher levels of government) and horizontal linkages (which can be of two types: between ministries at central level or between regions or communes). It is also true for linkages among various kinds of stakeholders – essentially public sector and private sector actors (profit or non-profit). In practice, these different forms of co-ordination can be integrated in one and the same system, as is the case for example with "micro-regions" in Mexico or the Czech Republic.

The vertical relation between the centre and regional government is crucial…
… Contracts provide one important means by which to formalise this relation…
… But co-ordination at the central level between ministries and departments is a pre-requisite to vertical integration of policy

Given the complexity of multi-level governance mechanisms, the main policy question is: what organisational or institutional devices can promote the active participation of central and regional levels of government in a co-operative rather than hierarchical system? This report examines one of the principal recent innovations that tries to respond to this question: the use of contractual arrangements among levels of government. Contractual arrangements across government levels represent a compromise, helping to reconcile the tendency towards decentralization with the responsibility of the central level to maintain overall coherence and consistency. Because they are negotiated, contract systems tend to be well-adapted to joint projects of regional development, more so than "automatic" fiscal equalisation mechanisms that often characterised traditional vertical relations. They also have some risks and drawbacks. These are mainly linked to the nature of the relationship among the partners, and have led to the introduction of incentives for the different parties to participate fully and to fulfil their contractual obligations. While some open questions remain, in general contract-based regional development should aim to:

1. ensure that local authorities are "empowered";
2. preserve the negotiating power of the central government with respect to other actors;
3. focus contractual arrangements on a limited number of key programmes, while leaving some room for local targeting;
4. ensure the transparency of the process and open the contractual negotiation to public participation, at least at some stages.

Only the central government can ensure co-ordinated action among the different actors, as a pre-requisite for the implementation of territorial policies of this type. This co-ordination can be achieved by means of dedicated agencies or through more flexible institutional mechanisms.

At regional and local level, closer horizontal co-operation offers significant cost and outcome advantages…

Closer co-operation among municipalities can be relevant from two perspectives: contributing to an improvement in the cost efficiency of local public services and improving the coherence and impact of development projects by emphasizing functional rather than administrative demarcations. Overall, voluntary associations appear to stand a greater chance of success than mergers ordered from the centre. Indeed, although they offer some clear advantages, the economic arguments in favour of mergers have not been proven.

… But this co-operation needs to be encouraged by the central level (rather than forced) and to be adapted to the specificity of the area

Co-operative solutions allow local authorities to preserve their identity and autonomy from an institutional point of view. Nonetheless, it is still necessary to find a workable compromise between the need for an intermediary organisation that manages joint programmes and the need to avoid over-complication of the local institutional structure. Moreover, the inter-municipal institutions often lack transparency. One solution is to make nomination of members of such inter municipal bodies more transparent.

Evaluations suggest that the elaboration of common, multi-sectoral development projects is more efficient than co-operation based on specialisation in the management and provision of one particular public service. This allows decision-making on economic development (which is by definition multi-sectoral) to be adapted to a more functional economic scale). Fiscal incentives from the central level and the adaptation of the type of inter-municipal coordination according to the characteristics of the area (metropolitan, urban/rural and remote areas) seem to encourage participation in such arrangements.

Better co-operation between border regions requires more local flexibility and giving a stronger say to local private actors

Interest in mechanisms for managing cross-border regions is the result of two distinct international trends: *first*, supra-national integration is reducing trade barriers between countries, and *second*, decentralisation is putting more power into the hands of subnational governments. Both trends increase the feasibility and potential benefits of collaboration across the border.

The approaches taken in Europe and in North America differ markedly. Despite their ambitious declarations, cross-border governments in Europe have often failed to reach regional development objectives. The cost of co-ordination and common decision making often appears to outweigh expected benefits. The dense institutional and policy networks that support cross-border co-operation have not automatically resulted in the establishment of new public-private alliances to address regional and local development issues. At its most successful, collaboration has worked mainly where public agencies have been strongly involved and had a direct say in project definition and implementation.

This differs somewhat from the pattern on the North American continent where governance structures tend to be more flexible, more oriented towards a few purposes, better able to react to specific problem situations and more driven by the private sector and local governments. North America's drive for regional integration is motivated much more by direct economic concerns.

Given the problems of motivating integration efforts in many cases, according greater weight to economic integration issues and allowing local private actors a stronger say in the direction that integration should take appears to be important.

The inclusion of private stakeholders, profit and non-profit, in the decision making and policy implementation processes contributes to improving the competitiveness of regions

Beyond closer collaboration between central and local governments, or between local or regional authorities, there is increasing recognition that purely public intervention has its limits, and this has opened the way for greater co-operation between the public and the private sector through public-private partnerships (PPP). The main traditional advantage that PPPs present is that they split the costs and risks of projects between the public and private sectors, tapping into the expertise and economies of scale available in the private sector that are rarely exploited for public policy. The principal risks associated with PPPs are linked to asymmetries of information and of commitment between the different parties of the agreements. These considerations have now to take into account more "inclusive" PPPs, of which the various local stakeholders of the development projects, profit and non profit, may contribute. From the perspective of public policy, some outstanding issues include:

- Local public authorities need guidance and, as far as is practicable, standardised processes for selecting and operating PPPs. This help does not only concern respect of competition regulations but also the steps to be followed to identify the best partner, evaluate the effectiveness of the PPP option, and diffuse information to other local jurisdictions, among other things.
- Local firms should be involved in PPPs devoted to local development. As users of collective services, they have views on their needs in terms of infrastructure, training, etc. And as suppliers of services, they will often be more attuned to improving outcomes than other actors that are less directly involved. Without infringing rules of competition, it would be worthwhile to provide them with the support and incentives necessary for them to participate in this way. This is particularly important with respect to SMEs. A similar logic should be applied with respect to citizen's groups and other non-profit organisations.

One of the most important challenges of the vertical and horizontal co-operation mechanisms is to enhance the competence of local actors

In order to obtain positive outcomes from these different innovations in the overall governance system, some element of capacity building needs to be emphasised. Examples include: change of civil servants, detachment of officials to private organisations, targeted training for local NGOs, and so on. The aim of these initiatives would be to increase the level of common practice and information exchange among the different actors participating in multi-level governance mechanisms.

At the same time, co-operative arrangements among levels of government and between public and private actors present in themselves important capacity building tools. An important recommendation is, therefore, that this aspect (empowerment as capacity building) should be emphasized from the outset, including clear definition of objectives and of the level of performance expected from participants.

... Another is to improve evaluation, including that of intangible outcomes

The question of the value added of co-operative arrangements in the organisation and delivery of public goods should be addressed. Cost-benefit assessment of the outcomes from physical investment can be taken into account, but this is insufficient. The intangible nature of many of the key factors relating to competitiveness, such as networking and interlinkages among actors, makes many performance indicators, such as share of local beneficiaries in the decisional boards, share of local and regional revenues from services offered to local firms, number of new companies advised by public or semi-public regional development agencies, etc., very unsatisfactory. These can supplement economic evaluation of the performance of technopoles or other investments, but do not address adequately the added value of the governance approach itself. This is particularly true with respect to the capacity building aspect that is implied in multi-level governance mechanisms.

In the case of multi-level partnerships, the evaluation problem needs to be addressed from the outset and an appropriate reporting system has to be established. Without such a framework, the financial incentives and sanctions that partnership and contract mechanisms often include are difficult to implement and to justify.

... And governments need to accept and encourage institutional experiments

In the absence of optimal solutions to the questions raised by the new objectives and instruments of regional policy, policymakers are obliged to experiment with what is practicable in the given context. In order for these experiments to be mainstreamed, where judged appropriate, it is important that the central government support a policy of encouraging and evaluating experimentation at regional level. Such a policy, based on, for example, grants for selected projects in competition, allows relevant innovations at local level to be diffused more widely.

ISBN 92-64-00946-9
Building Competitive Regions
Strategies and Governance
© OECD 2005

Part I

Strategies

1. Competitiveness in a regional context

The changing nature of regional policy in OECD countries

The significance accorded to competitiveness by policymakers reflects the increasing emphasis on competitive advantage for national economies. Policy makers across the OECD stress that their countries must become more "competitive" if they are to maintain their economic position *vis-à-vis* other industrial or developing nations and regions and respond to challenges such as perceived productivity gaps, competition for mobile investment, rapid adoption of new technology and electronic commerce. While the wording and emphasis vary, the definitions originating from governmental and non-governmental sources tend to share some fundamental elements and assumptions. First, improving competitiveness at micro or firm level is a means by which to improve macro-economic performance. Second, benefits from improved firm competitiveness can be translated into better living standards for all. Spillover effects transfer benefits from growth in one area to another with which it is geographically linked or with which it has close economic ties. Third, competition takes place in, and is "tested" by, open (international) market conditions – it can be thought of as "relative productivity in traded sectors". And, finally, places compete with each other, in the same way that firms do, for "market share".[1]

Increasingly, the concept of competitiveness is extended to the regional level. The argument is that (some) firms gain general and specific advantages from geographical proximity to material inputs (raw materials, land, etc.), to suppliers, to markets, to transport infrastructure, and so on. It follows that places have different endowments and degrees of attractiveness. Michael Storper formulates regional competitiveness as the capacity of a region to attract and maintain successful firms while maintaining stable or rising standards of living for the region's inhabitants. Skilled labour and investment gravitate away from "uncompetitive" regions towards more competitive ones. The term "structural competitiveness" is often used to describe this capacity of a region to support and attract economic activities. "Territorial capital" has also been used to describe the bundle of attributes that a region possesses that make it more or less competitive with respect to other regions.

The extension of the competitiveness concept to the regional level is recent, but is having a major influence on the direction of policy. In particular, it is supporting a revival of interest in a new form of regional policy. Regional policy began in most OECD countries in the 1950s and 1960s, a period of relatively strong economic growth, fiscal expansion and low unemployment. The principal objective of the measures that were introduced was greater equity. The main instruments used were wealth redistribution through financial transfers by the national government accompanied by large-scale public investments. During the 1970s and early 1980s, successive economic shocks and changes in the global economy led to the emergence of geographical concentrations of unemployment in many countries, and regional policy evolved rapidly to address this new challenge. In the earlier period, the focus was on reducing disparities (in income, in infrastructure stock, etc.). Now an additional focus on employment creation was added. The guiding theoretical assumption in this case was that public policy could alter supply conditions (essentially by changing production cost factors through production subsidies and incentives) and thereby influence industrial (re)location decisions, both with respect to existing firms and new investments.

Overall, the results of these policies were disappointing: regional disparities have not reduced significantly, appearing as entrenched as ever in many countries. At a regional level, the success of these policies in restructuring the economic base of the target areas has also been limited. Attraction of inward investment illustrates the limitations that regional policies came up against. Many governments have attempted to attract FDI into target regions, with, as a premier objective, creation of employment, but also an assumption that spillovers would benefit local enterprises, principally increasing their technological and organisational capacity. However, numerous studies have found that in most cases the facilities brought into the region accrue little for the local economy in terms of productivity gains among local enterprises. Often, these branch plants are weakly embedded in local production systems, generating very low levels of local supplier linkages. Most foreign-owned subsidiaries show weak innovation tendencies, and very few conduct R&D or have linkages with the local innovation system, preferring to retain their R&D in their main country of origin (Pavitt and Patel, 1991). The experience of Scotland's so-called "Silicon Glen" is a good example. Over the course of the 1970s and 1980s a large number of high-technology companies located in Scotland, among them IBM, Hewlett Packard, Motorola, NEC and Compaq. These companies created large numbers of jobs and the inward investment strategy was successful in moving Scotland away from reliance on declining heavy industries. By 1990, electronics manufacturing accounted for 20% of all manufacturing and 42% of exports. This policy was supported through large-scale incentives with electronics manufacturers in Scotland receiving half of the available regional selective assistance grants over the period 1995-1999. Nonetheless, the linkage between foreign-owned and local firms has not lived up to expectations; for example, locally sourced inputs were only a very small proportion of total inputs. Moreover, the local input tended to be mainly at the low-tech end – packaging, plastics, rubber and metal components, for example.

Over the course of the 1980s and 1990s, regional policy moved down the political agenda. Large allocations for these programmes became unsustainable in a period of successive economic recessions, generalised higher levels of unemployment and increasing pressure on public expenditure. In response to poor outcomes, regional policy has evolved and is evolving from a top-down, subsidy based group of interventions designed to reduce regional disparities into a much broader "family" of policies designed to improve regional competitiveness and characterised by: 1) a strategic concept or development strategy that covers a wide range of direct and indirect factors that affect the performance of local firms; 2) a focus on endogenous assets, and less on exogenous investments and transfers; 3) an emphasis on opportunity rather than on disadvantage; and 4) a collective/negotiated governance approach involving national, regional and local government plus other stakeholders, with the central government taking a less dominant role. Evidence of this so-called "paradigm shift" in regional policy can be seen in recent reforms of regional policy in a number of OECD countries. For example, signs that the local linkages were not likely to increase, but if anything more prone to decrease, has led Scotland's development agency, Scottish Enterprise, to rethink its strategy and embark on a development strategy (*Smart Successful Scotland*) that emphasises the importance of innovation, human capital and the competitiveness of indigenous business. A similar process has taken place in Ireland, another region that was successful in attracting FDI but that is now reorienting its strategy (*Enterprise 2010 Ireland*).

Diagnosing competitive advantage and identifying policy options

Developing strategies that will have an impact on the competitiveness of a given region involves identifying the sources or potential sources of the region's competitive advantage. As such, an extremely wide range of factors could be targets for policy. Some of these factors are national or international in nature and lie beyond the scope of regional strategies, while others appear more open to influence or replication at regional level.

Many factors that affect the functioning of enterprises or that encourage investment are regulated through national policies that do not differentiate among regions, i.e., that are based on legislative or regulatory frameworks that are space-neutral. For example: the Intellectual Property Rights (IPR) regime affects incentives to undertake research and product development. Many of the special development zones that have been introduced around the world

> **Box 1.1. Targeted regulatory reform initiatives: Japan's Special Zones**
>
> A major initiative that exemplifies the close links between territorial policy and regulatory reform is the Programme of Special Zones for Regulatory Reform. The objective of this programme is to stimulate private sector activity by exploiting targeted regulatory reforms that remove specific, localised development obstacles. The Zones are designated by local entities (mainly governmental but also local consortia) on the basis of an assessment of the geographical area that would benefit directly from revision of a particular national regulation or law. The underlying assumption is that many of the bottlenecks in the Japanese economy are localised and that relaxing national regulatory frameworks in certain specific cases could give a boost to both local and national economies. The philosophy of the programme is based on the assertion that local actors are best placed to define their needs in terms of special exemptions or special treatment. The national government presents no model in advance and local groups must compete with other localities to prove that their proposal will have both local and national impacts. Local actors must organise themselves before submitting a proposal, and whatever strains or pressures might be caused by the implementation of special measures in the zones (*e.g.*, with respect to adjacent areas where the measures are not applicable or balancing different interest groups) must be mediated/negotiated locally. As such, the programme is promoting the capacity building, local autonomy and horizontal co-operation mechanisms that decentralisation processes are trying to instil.

include measures to accord exemptions from specific regulations for firms located within the target area. Region-specific regulatory frameworks have also been tested in some countries as a means by which to overcome localised market failures and/or test the feasibility of more general, nationwide reform (see Box 1.1).

Factors relating to the geographical location, endowments and features of every region are also undeniably important. Often, these can be harnessed by policy – for example, development policies may seek to capitalise on a region's locational advantages as a transport hub or its position at a national border – but these assets usually cannot be replicated and, as such, lie beyond the scope of public policy. In addition to geographical location, these factors could also include the presence of raw materials (such as oil or minerals) that support extractive industries. It is fair to assume that many geographical and physical endowments are becoming less significant as transportation times and costs reduce. Nonetheless, there are many regions for which their principal comparative advantage remains "endowment"-based. A 1998 survey of OECD rural regions confirmed that a large number of the most successful rural regions possessed features of this type.

Leaving aside these categories of non-replicable input factors, OECD work suggests that there are two basic groups of factors that can be influenced by policy: 1) those directly related to economic activities (principally related to economies of agglomeration) and 2) those that have an indirect influence on economic activities (principally related to what have been termed economies of "urbanisation").

1) *Direct*: Individual firms derive comparative advantage from their internal organisation, management style, internal processes of innovation, product development, marketing, and so on. In some regions, the performance of the local economy is driven by a few dynamic firms. In many other regions, collective characteristics pertaining to groups of firms or sectors provide a source of productivity gain. These collective advantages – often found in clusters or productive systems – stem from the historical development of local sectors and links with the region, firm size and structure, level of specialisation (agglomeration effects related to specialisation of industrial production, and any spillovers such as high innovation capacity and concentration of specialised workers), use of advanced technologies, and the use of networking as a business practice.

2) *Indirect*: The wider business environment at regional level includes a range of factors that either encourage or inhibit business activity. These include the efficiency of the transport and communications infrastructure, the level of local taxes and the quality of public services that they fund, provision of affordable housing, the presence and quality of education institutions. This is strongly linked to the strategic management of the economy and the level of leadership that local authorities provide and, within that, the approach taken to support local business, attract new industries and to provide an environment that is attractive for investors and employees. In general, attention focuses on the framework conditions for business, the tangible factors that increase or decrease production costs – local tax regimes, transport infrastructures, and so on. However, there is increasing recognition that environmental quality, social stability and other attributes, often derived from good local governance, can have an important influence on regional competitiveness.

In order to define policy strategies that are relevant for the regional context as well as fitting national policy objectives and constraints, it is essential to move from the listing of potential contributory factors, to an approach that sets priorities, assesses causal relationships in the regional economy, etc. A series of reviews undertaken by OECD confirm the central

Box 1.2. **Region type and competitiveness strategy: some examples**

1) Knowledge activity oriented city regions. An innovation-oriented strategy has been a key element in the success of the Helsinki, Öresund, Seoul and Montreal regions, and is the aspiration and main policy preoccupation for other regions reviewed such as Glasgow and Melbourne. These large metropolitan or city-regions have similar combinations of large population, good infrastructure, educational facilities, strong demand in international and national services, etc. The competitiveness policy issue for such regions is how these assets are managed in order to have an impact on relative competitiveness.

2) City regions in transition: There are a large number of smaller city regions, often with a strong industrial tradition, high quality infrastructure and even prestigious research capabilities but specialised in declining sectors. Such cities and regions are looking for their niche with respect to high growth/high rent "knowledge activity oriented" regions. Of the regions reviewed, this category would include Newcastle, Belfast, Champagne-Ardenne and Bergamo. In these regions, the endogenous assets of the region are strong, but are poorly adapted to current economic conditions. Competitiveness policies emphasise transformation of labour force skills and industrial specialisations, including stronger roles for the region's educational institutions.

3) Specialised manufacturing regions. Other regions, often with moderate population densities but dense infrastructure networks achieve critical mass in a limited number of economic sectors. This category includes the Central Valencia Districts, Modena, Siena (as well as other regions identified in the national reviews of Italy and France) and is the preferred trajectory for Canberra. These regions depend on their ability to absorb and apply new knowledge and adapt to international pressures through an enterprise structure that emphasises positive feed-backs among economic actors (research, government and local and foreign firms). The issue for such regions is to maintain and enhance the relational assets that support their high productivity.

4) Rural regions. Finally, there are regions where neither population and infrastructure nor particular forms of firm organisation offer opportunities for external economies or above average rents. The extreme examples of this category are remote rural regions, such as the regions of Tzoumerka and Teruel, but also applies to regions without strong geographical handicaps, such as Moravska Trebova-Jericka, until such time as physical and knowledge infrastructure are upgraded. The endogenous assets of these regions are less clear. Nonetheless, evolutions in the demand for rural areas, and more specifically the demand for rural amenities, promise to increase the value of the environmental assets of rural areas.

importance of competitiveness issues for regions and the interest of policymakers at both national and regional level in identifying strategies. The series of regional reviews suggest that a small number of generic success factors appear repeatedly in dynamic regions, constitute the principal aspirations of intermediate regions or appear as weaknesses in less dynamic regions. These reviews suggest a very broad typology of regions, implying related but different policy needs (see Box 1.2).

The next two sections will assess the initiatives that member governments have introduced in order to increase the competitiveness of regions, focusing on 1) policies and instruments to increase the competitiveness/productivity of firms and 2) policies and instruments to improve the quality of the region as a business location.

2. Competitive firms: policies to generate innovation and knowledge

The competitive advantage of regions: exploiting proximity and linkages to generate innovation

The search for a new approach to regional industrial policy in mature economies is now mainly focused on making domestic firms more competitive, and this has, in turn, led to an emphasis on innovation and better use of the knowledge and technology available within a region. On the one hand, the reorientation of regional policy in many countries has led to a more sophisticated awareness of regional innovation systems and their components. On the other hand, science and technology policymakers are taking increasing account of the importance of region-specific factors – in particular the role of proximity – in the innovation process. This approach emphasises the importance of agglomeration effects for knowledge creation and diffusion and takes the view that the regional level is the most appropriate to assure knowledge a favourable "diffusive" environment. Physical proximity, and the shared 'regional culture' that often comes with it – *i.e.* shared practices, attitudes, expectations that facilitate the flow and sharing of tacit and other forms of proprietary knowledge – have become the cornerstones of an implicitly "regional" system of innovation.

The relation between innovation and region-level interaction is supported by a large body of academic literature. A string of observations in the 1980s, from clustering of hi-tech firms to the rising competitiveness of more traditional industrial districts, triggered the idea of a new form of spatial-industrial organisation.[2] The regional version of the innovation system developed by Porter provides an illustrative and very influential example. According to Porter, "regions compete in providing the most productive environment. It is not the industry that matters but the way the firm competes, its use of the advantages that the local environment brings.

Porter's much-cited development "diamond" structure contains four principal factors: 1) a supportive context for firm strategy and rivalry (i.e., policies/regulations that encourage investment and technical upgrading); 2) robust demand conditions (a core of advanced, competitive and demanding customers); 3) related and supporting industries (capable local suppliers, preferably organised in clusters); and 4) good factor/input conditions (human resources, physical infrastructure, etc.). The system should be animated by dynamic, open competition among locally based rivals (Porter, 1994 and 1990).

While the model has been criticised for being inflexible, it provides an illustration of how innovative capacity can drive the competitiveness of a place, based of the ability of that region to exploit its own resources. The work of Storper has also been influential in promoting the view that it is a basket of "untraded interdependencies" (labour markets, regional conventions, norms and values, public or semi-public institutions, etc.)[3] that foster an environment conducive to trust, co-operation and innovation, often synonymous with social capital. The corollary of this argument is that lack of such untraded interdependencies is typical of many vulnerable regions, including, notably in the context of debate over exogenous vs. endogenous development models, those characterised by loosely embedded branch plants (Cooke et al, 2004). The same concept of locational advantage has been used by other theorists to focus attention on the crucial role of "geographical cumulative causation" and "positive feed-backs" (Kaldor and others, including Krugman), "knowledge workers" (Moss Kanter, 1995; Reich, 1991) and "systems of innovation" (Lundvall and Johnson, 1994), as well as the embeddedness of investment in generating competitive advantages (Dunning, 1992). There is some evidence to support these theories. Recent work by Cooke (2004a) on the biosciences industry, for example, reveals a close association between proximity and knowledge transfer. Cooke finds that in regions where bioscience firms are strongly embedded in regional networks, companies perform better than in other regions.

In their search for operational instruments to increase the intensity of interactions among innovation and knowledge generators and users, regional policymakers have developed a wide range of instruments. Overall, three broad (and not mutually exclusive) categories of policy measures stand out:

1. **Real estate based projects:** Development of science parks, technopoles and other industrial spaces designed to facilitate networking and technology development and transfer through "co-location".

2. **Relational asset/cluster policies.** Initiatives to support existing or nascent groupings of firms with collective services and other measures to build co-operation within the cluster and to enable joint initiatives to export, market, etc.

3. **Linking research and industry.** Linking knowledge producers with users; systems of technology and innovation diffusion; commercialisation of innovation, including specific models such as science parks, technical service centres and technical education institutions.

Constructing proximity: science parks, technopoles and other real estate instruments

Among the longest established policy instruments for promoting regional research and innovation capacity is the creation of high-tech industrial spaces, which are intended to provide a supportive business location for innovative firms. The development of technopoles and science parks goes back to the success of market-driven technology agglomerations like Silicon Valley and Route 128. The success of these regions made them best practice examples that other regions tried to imitate. A wave of publicly supported technopoles emerged in the 1970s and 1980s, with ambitious targets and correspondingly big sites and budgets – Research Triangle in North Carolina and Sophia Antipolis in France are two well-known examples. These triggered a variety of more modest adaptations of the model, tailored to the means of the regions adopting them. The fact that firms like Apple and Hewlett Packard grew up in such environments has certainly added credence to the theory that co-location is beneficial for innovative small firms.

Locating together benefits firms and can provide a focus for FDI and entrepreneurship

The rationale underlying the creation of shared industrial space is that physical proximity between specialised firms, and between enterprises and other technological organisations, combined with appropriate organisational arrangements to facilitate cross-fertilisation, will lead to better generation and exploitation of technological creativity. The following general models have emerged:

- large technopoles, established by national governments as part of a combination spatial planning and innovation policy, to attract external (often large) investors in high-tech centres and to locate (public) research centres;
- science parks linked to a university, often developed at a regional or metropolitan level, with university involvement in park management, with a major objective to encourage spin-outs;
- stand-alone science parks, developed by regional or local authorities as a local incubator area for SMEs and to attract high-tech investments;
- incubator centres, a building complex with space for independent SMEs. (Longhi and Quéré, 1997; 236).

Initially, many of these were the result of national policy initiatives designed to create poles of growth, either to consolidate advanced regions or to diffuse high end economic activity to non-core regions. France and Japan, for example, have been at the forefront of this type of growth pole policy. The prime objectives were to attract high-tech investments and skilled workers to target areas. To provide some impetus, most technopoles involved the relocation or creation of public research facilities or even universities, and were sometimes linked to policies focused on sectors in which state procurement played a dominant role: defence, aerospace, nuclear and electronic technologies, for example. Some technopoles were also built around investments by major multinational enterprises. An example is ZIRST in Grenoble, France, where three major electronic firms – Thompson, Merlin-Gerin and Hewlett-Packard – were major early stage investors. Recently, the role of regional and local governments has increased dramatically. The interest of regional and local authorities in projects that imitate the large-scale nationally-driven science parks has led to some spectacular flops, but also to a refinement of the smaller-scale version of the technopole as a workable and locally fundable concept.

Technology parks and similar initiatives are often seen as a vehicle for attracting FDI to locations where links can be developed with local suppliers and research institutions. Foreign investment is assumed to produce significant spillovers to the local business sector.[4] The spillovers are assumed to be more intense and more rapid where firms are located in the same facility and are involved in organised networking as is often the case in science parks and similar. Technopoles and science parks also often emphasise incubation functions and entrepreneurship, with many of the larger initiatives including a business incubator. The aim is mainly to incite spin offs from larger firms, with support services provided for the new business at below market rates. The ability of the technology park to effectively fulfil this role depends to a large extent on whether specialised services and support staff are available.[5]

Outcomes require long-term commitment and institutional co-operation

Assessing the overall impact of these initiatives, it appears that the most effective technopoles share three main features:

- some basic "raw materials" or framework conditions, notably a specialised research domain, dynamic manufacturing and service companies, higher education facilities, and finance and human resources;
- mechanisms for cross-fertilisation, comprising organisational and communication initiatives that support a culture of collaboration within the technopole; and

I. STRATEGIES

- an added value element involving the emergence and use of new technological knowledge, the creation of new products and processes, the creation of durable and stable jobs, or the arrival of new enterprises,

It is clear that many of the varieties of technopole or science park do not possess or emphasise all of these features. On this basis, we can distinguish between two types of initiative:

- *real technopoles*: which are more comprehensive and ambitious measures that include all three features (examples include the market-led US cases, the French technopoles process and individual cases in Europe and Asia); and
- *quasi-technopoles*: to denote the less comprehensive initiatives that would typically downplay the networking and cross-fertilisation aspect of the technopole concept and that are essentially industrial parks, business support or information centres.

The fact that so many technopoles are found in the latter "quasi-technopole" category is partly because, unlike some other regional innovation approaches, they involve development of a physical site. In general, the construction part of the intervention is easy to design and is a tangible political achievement. The cross fertilisation and value added aspects are, however, much more complicated to generate, slow to emerge, difficult to measure and, as a result, difficult to fund. In many cases, the crucial cross-fertilisation dynamic is relatively weak and other objectives, notably attraction of FDI have a more central importance. As noted above, they appear to work best when the "raw materials" of the system are already in place, such as a highly regarded R&D centre or some co-location of linked industries. In these cases, the public investment aims simply to enhance existing patterns of activity. In the majority of situations, however, the baseline conditions need to be up-graded, and this requires long-term investment and commitment. The case of Sophia-Antipolis, a prominent French technopole, illustrates the point (see Box 1.3).

Given the long-term nature of the investment, the key questions for policymakers include:

- is the clustering imposed by the technology park an effective means of cross fertilisation and innovation diffusion?
- is the technology park destined to be a high tech enclave or can it be the mainspring for a broader regional development strategy as well?

With respect to these questions, the record of both fully-fledged and quasi technology parks is mixed. Although, in theory, technology parks can form an essential interface between inter-regional and international systems, many have been criticised as expensive oases, "cathedrals in the desert",

> ### Box 1.3. **Sophia-Antipolis: slow evolution**
>
> Sophia-Antipolis, located close to Nice, is today counted as a major European technopole. It covers 2 300 hectares, 800 of which are given over to economic activity. Sophia-Antipolis is unusual in the sense that it was set up in a region without an industrial or university tradition; the region's only resources were linked to its main activity, tourism. These were an international airport, transport infrastructure, good climate, and a cosmopolitan tradition. These initial conditions, important for an understanding of how the place developed, turned out in the end to be favourable.
>
> Two phases can be identified in the development of Sophia-Antipolis. Up until the beginning of the 1990s, Sophia-Antipolis grew by accumulating external resources. The project benefited from the French policy of decentralisation, becoming the home for the technology centres of major French businesses, and also from the multinationalisation that went on in the 1970s and 1980s, the time when American companies set their sights on the European market. A number of public research laboratories were also set up there, as well as higher education facilities, which contributed to the emergence of a highly-qualified labour market. This exogenous development proved to be perfectly suited to the needs of these businesses, which were adapting their products to a new market. That model underwent a crisis in the 1990s. Sophia-Antipolis was able to generate a new, endogenous, development model based on its accumulated resources. By contrast with the first phase in which public policy had played a major role, this time it was the actors that generated the new model through different associations of businesses (Telecom Valley for instance, which includes all the actors involved in ICT and which has enabled numerous exchanges to take place). Telecommunications, and more especially the technologies associated with the mobile phone, developed into one of the fundamental local areas of competence. Growth no longer comes from attracting exogenous resources but from the development of local businesses and technologies.
>
> Source: Longhi C. (1999); and Garnsey E. and C. Longhi (2004).

attracting the lion's share of regional public investment without contributing sufficiently to the local economy.

Overall, technology parks appear to have performed best in three types of region:

- *Old industrial regions,* which within the framework of industrial reconversion have sought to create technopoles as a way of changing their overall image,

to attract new economic activities and to modernise the local industrial fabric;
- *Urban locations* offering economies of scale, a strong concentration of high technology based activities and the possible transition between traditional and new technologies;
- *Some new industrial regions*, where initiatives have capitalised on the emergence of dynamic companies, particularly in high-tech sectors, in areas with little industrial tradition.

Reducing the size and ambitions of such initiatives in an effort to tailor them to less suitable locations or to more restricted budgets seems an inappropriate development model.

Implementation and management of technopoles also poses a number of significant challenges that relate to governance:

- The construction of a technology park goes beyond the designated site and involves the development of support infrastructures of different kinds, such as highway extensions, public transportation links, etc. These require close linkage of regional innovation strategies with other investment programmes that may have different overall objectives, timeframes, etc.
- Many technology parks involve greenfield developments or anticipate the extension of existing sites into greenfield sites. These new developments will have environmental impacts, impacts on transport flows and even impacts on residential location. As such, they can have region-wide implications, and as such should be the object of close inter-municipal and inter-regional co-ordination;
- In order to reap the benefits associated with "real" technopoles, a substantial investment over a long period is required. This investment will inevitably involve national, regional and sometimes supranational funding sources from a variety of sectoral budgets. For example, technology parks based on existing universities will often involve a transformation and upgrading of the research capacity/focus of the regional university – this will require support for R&D activities through national R&D budgets and programmes.

Building relational assets: cluster policies

Research studies of advanced urban, intermediate and rural regions often emphasise the importance of specialisation in productive activities where a competitive advantage can be derived and maintained. Others argue, on the contrary, that specialisation by a region in a limited range of sectors is a dangerous strategy and that diversity is the real key to creativity and innovation. Rather than specialising in specific sectors or even product types, the advocates of clusters argue that they promote specialisation in a complex array of related activities demanding diverse and highly market-oriented skills. Interest in clusters arises, therefore, because of the potential of innovative clusters to offer the benefits associated with specialisation at regional level with flexibility and resistance to adverse changes in market conditions.

Another motivation for interest in clusters is the accumulation of evidence from different countries that both productivity and wage levels can be higher in clustered activities than in non-clustered activities, and that clusters in "traded" (as opposed to local or resource dependent) industries have a strong influence on the overall prosperity of the region and on its average wage level. Porter finds that clusters increase the contribution of traded sectors to regional output and wages. Similar research by METI in Japan and the Bank of Italy has suggested a correlation between clusters and higher productivity. Research into the sources of this productivity advantage focuses principally on the positive impact of the circulation of people and knowledge around a local economic system on the generation of innovative ideas and the development of new products and technologies. Within dynamic high-technology clusters, levels of personal exchanges between firms appear to be higher than in non-clustered locations. This type of "cross-pollination" of ideas and innovation is put forward as one of the main drivers of the success of the Silicon Valley model (Saxenian, 1994). Some research seems to empirically verify this thesis. For example, the successful Stockholm ICT cluster exhibits higher rates of inter-firm labour mobility that the rest of the labour market and higher rates of intra-firm mobility than other comparable private-sector enterprises (Power and Lundmark, 2004).

At the same time, other studies have questioned the validity of the cluster hypothesis, asserting that problems of definition and measurement make empirical evaluation of the relative performance of clusters and, in particular, the origins of any difference with non-clustered industries statistically dubious (Martin and Sunley, 2003). What is certain is that much of the evidence to support the view that clusters are more productive is case specific and large scale empirical reviews are extremely rare, with the review of the Bank of Italy standing out as the most extensive research effort (the problem from an international perspective being that Italy already provides the best evidence of external economies derived from clustering). Other researchers have found that clusters tend to be strong in only certain parts of the production process or in particular sectors or sub-sectors, further questioning the assertion that clusters can be a generalisable model of economic organisation or an appropriate target for public policy.

In practice: an approach that forms a key element of regional strategies

The "classic" Italian example of established industrial clusters and supportive policy environments has been widely cited for some time. More recently, cases such as Helsinki where clusters seem not to have been purely a historical development but a phenomenon influenced by public policy have led national and regional policymakers to focus on the strategies that can encourage this type of agglomeration and network building. The reversal of fortunes of Helsinki has provided a convincing example of how clusters can turn a regional economy around. Helsinki has developed, very rapidly, a strong specialisation in a high growth sector, and has been extremely successful as a result. One of the appealing lessons of the Helsinki case is that while sectoral mix owes much to chance and path dependency has an influence, insightful public policy undoubtedly played a role. Box 1.4 describes how a recently introduced national cluster development programme in Japan was inspired at least in part by the success of a publicly supported but locally driven network in a Tokyo suburb.

Cluster policies have proliferated over the past decade, with manifestations ranging from policies to encourage low-resourced, small-group business networks without a particular sectoral focus to complex, large-scale programmes of co-ordinated measures that target a specific, geographically-cohesive industry. As an approach to regional development, they differ from traditional incentive-based regional development policies by concentrating their support on networks of diverse agents rather than on individual firms. Although there has been some questioning of the degree to which cluster policies are more than a reformulation of traditional sectoral policies (Raines 2002), they are widely regarded as innovative in bringing together formerly separate policy elements (Benneworth et al., 2003):

> "Cluster policies have taken the sectoral focus and industry-specific measures from industrial policy; an awareness that regional economic growth is dependent on the interaction of businesses, institutions (such as universities) and wider environmental factors such as the labour market and infrastructure from regional development policies; and … have acknowledged the importance of developing the capacity of individual (particularly smaller) businesses to overcome their growth challenges from SME policy…"

Benneworth et al. (2003) consider that these policy measures can be subdivided into three groups: 1) support for existing clusters; 2) support for businesses that already collaborate; and 3) establishment of new collaborations between non-cooperating businesses. The first-step, therefore, for most regions is to understand precisely the economic and "relational" geography of the region. Many large regions have undertaken audits of their

Box 1.4. **Cluster development: a national approach and a regional model in Japan**

The TAMA network

The area of TAMA is in a suburb of Tokyo and became industrialised as enterprises moved out of inner city and costal areas, partly due to the Factory Restriction Laws, to find less congested areas for industrial location. The area developed a strong accumulation of sub-contracting enterprises in the electronics, transportation, precision machinery and other technologically advanced branches. As large firms moved overseas or contracted their operations during the 1990s, the smaller firms located in the TAMA region lost a substantial part of their customer base. The association focuses on the revitalisation and development of industries located in the western parts of the Tokyo metropolis, creating new technologies, products and businesses. The association promotes industry interaction and seeks to strengthen traditionally poor industry-university linkages through exchange and joint R&D projects, with the broader goal of creating synergies that will foster new technological development and commercialisation. TAMA has established a Technology Licensing Office to assist in patenting, licensing, and R&D commercialisation. TAMA founders report that they have been successful in raising the concerns of companies in these sectors to policy makers, in catalysing academic-industry links (important because many of the region's universities are small and not experienced in technology transfer), and in creating a unifying hub in an otherwise fragmented region.

Japan's Industrial Cluster programme

A 1996 White Paper on SMEs noted that firms with the characteristics of those in the TAMA region could maintain their competitiveness through networking with other similar producers and with research generators such as universities and labs. Partly inspired by the success of TAMA, the Japanese Ministry for Economy, Trade and Industry (METI) Industrial Clusters Programme, introduced in 2001, endeavours to build on the specific structural assets of 19 regions. Officials of the Regional Bureaus of Economy, Trade and Industry (approximately 500 persons) work with approximately 5,800 local small and medium enterprises and with researchers of more than 220 universities to implement measures in three main fields: 1) giving support to exchanges and co-operation between industry, academia, and government; 2) giving support to the development of technologies for practical use based on regional characteristics; and 3) establishment of facilities to provide training to entrepreneurs. In addition, a relatively large number of local governments participate in the METI Industrial Cluster Programme. Given that much of the financing within these clusters is local funding, the attitude and capacity of local government to take a more pro-active role in enterprise policy will also be crucial.

Source: OECD Territorial Review of Japan (2005)

> ### Box 1.5. **Cluster audit in Montreal**
>
> The first task for policy makers is to identify the key characteristics of clusters and understand their different dynamics and potentials. This work is being undertaken in Montreal through the *Stratégie métropolitaine de développement économique par créneaux d'excellence*. Montreal's economy is based on strong specialisation in a number of sectors. The preliminary research phase identified 15 possible clusters to focus on in Greater Montreal: agriculture/bio-food, professional and business services, tourism/leisure, aerospace, information technology, life sciences, nanotechnology, metals and metal products, fashion/textiles, transportation/distribution, plastics, composite materials, printing/publishing, chemicals, and environmental industries. These were divided into three categories: existing/traditional clusters, emerging clusters and diffused clusters (those not geographically concentrated). As this list suggests, there is no shortage of possible employment sectors in the Montreal economy on which to build. The problem is weaving the multiple strengths of the regional economy into a cohesive whole.
>
> The point of departure in the case of Montreal is that the strategy should take a metropolitan-region perspective. Unless cluster initiatives are specifically structured to engage actors throughout the Metropolitan region, they run the risk of heightening the tensions that exist between smaller municipalities in the region and the new mega-city of Montreal itself. A second principle of the cluster strategy is that it should address problems of duplication among institutions, streamlining interventions according to an agreed set of priorities. Given the potential for conflict between proponents of specific locations or specific institutions, it is important that the process of identifying priority clusters and priority measures is both transparent and focused. In this respect, the initiative to engage a working group to elaborate a development strategy based on clusters "of excellence", appears to be an important step forward. While there is a great deal of activity around the different clusters – various cluster-based associations and committees – there has not been until now an overview of the range of clusters in the metropolitan region that both diagnosed strengths and weaknesses and proposed concerted policy action. The ultimate aim of the group is to follow an open methodology by which the diagnostic is verified and leads to agreed conclusions of the policy actions that the diagnosis implies in the context of the level and type of public investment available.
>
> *Source:* OECD *Territorial Reviews* of Montreal (2004).

economic structure in order to specifically identify groupings of firms that could be the target for collective support. The example (Box 1.5) describes an ongoing process in Montreal, a city with strong industrial specialisations in aeronautics and pharmaceuticals that is looking to establish a more comprehensive cluster development strategy that takes into account not only different categories of existing clusters but also identifies new opportunities.

Unlike the development of regional technology centres or science parks, cluster policies require relatively low capital investment. Nonetheless, as both national and regional governments have discovered, they tend to be human resource intensive and demand a significant commitment of time on the part of both the public policy officers and specialised brokers/facilitators, making the overall funding requirement significant. The Scottish case provides a good example (see Box 1.6).

Policy measures tend to focus on providing common resources for groups of inter-related firms – such as specialised infrastructure or specific skills training programmes – or to encourage linkages between and amongst firms

---

Box 1.6. Cluster policies: success involves intensive effort: the case of Scotland

Scotland has several existing and emerging enterprise clusters, characterised by strong linkages and networks between firms, the presence of specialised supporting institutions and infrastructure and well-developed sector labour markets. Scottish Enterprise was one of the first economic development agencies to consider the potential of the cluster approach, with research undertaken in 1993 to identify Scotland's clusters and to assess which could benefit from specifically targeted support. Critically, Scottish Enterprise did not seek to create entirely new clusters of firms. Instead it prioritised clusters that demonstrated strong existing capacity, willingness from industry players to work together and with the public sector and where there was the potential for policy to make a difference.

This is an example of a successful regional cluster-based policy managed through a development agency. At the same time, it should be noted that this approach was supported with significant funding and has been resource intensive from the beginning. It was supported with EUR 360 million over six years. The process of working out how public policy can help to generate linkages among firms and between firms and other actors was long and painstaking. The results obtained have justified the investment, but they also suggest that the cluster audit represents a crucial first step before this strategy is taken forward.

Source: OECD, *Urban Renaissance: Glasgow* (2002).

and research providers. The target group of these services should be groups of firms rather than a single firm. A survey of research on support for clusters identified a series of actions that have proven to be successful in one or more places (Rosenfeld, 2002):

- Regional economic analysis and benchmarking to better understand how the regional economy functions as a system and which policy levers are likely to have the greatest impact. Actions: identification of clusters; modelling and mapping of systemic relationships; benchmarking of clusters against competitors.
- Engagement with the collective needs of employers and institutions. Actions: recognition, or where unmet need exists, creation of cluster associations; formalisation of communication channels; fostering of inter-firm collaboration.
- Organisation and delivery of services around the complexities and interdependencies of business needs, rather than individual generic functions. Actions: organisation and dissemination of cluster-oriented information; establishment of one-stop cluster hubs; formation of cross-agency cluster teams; creation of cluster branches of government; facilitation of external connections.
- Building a specialised workforce, with the aim of producing workers who are more productive, informed about labour markets and better connected to employers. Actions: qualification of people for employment; use of clusters as context for learning; establishment of cluster skill centres; formation of partnerships between educational institutions and clusters; support for regional skills alliances; working with NGOs to reach low-income populations.
- Allocation and attraction of resources and investment to maximise impacts on the economy. Actions: incentives or purpose-specific funds for multi-firm projects only; investment in cluster R&D; support for applications for national and EU funding in less-favoured regions; funding of critical foundation factors (*e.g.* education, healthcare, housing).
- Stimulation of innovation and entrepreneurship to generate new ideas and new enterprises. Actions: investment in innovations and business start-ups; support for cluster-based incubators; facilitation of entrepreneurs' support networks; promotion of innovation networks; building of technology cluster hubs.
- Marketing and branding of the region. Actions: targeting of inward investment; promotion of clusters; formation of export networks; exploiting opportunities for regional branding.

These services can be provided by a variety of different actors, government, quasi-government or private, each having certain advantages. Legitimacy in building consensus, for example, may favour governmental agencies or associations. The same is true when services imply disclosure of sensitive information or brokering between potentially conflicting interests: public or collective actors may be perceived as offering better guarantees of neutrality and confidentiality. The need for specialised skills, on the other hand, could argue in favour of private sector provision. The risk, particularly in more advanced regions, is that many of the services that cluster policies promote could well be provided through the market by the same private actors. In regions with a less dense "knowledge infrastructure", however, this kind of specialised private provider might be more difficult to find.

Diversity of contexts and policy approaches makes evaluation of outcomes difficult

Interest in cluster development has arisen mainly because of positive outcomes in industrial districts in Italy and in high-tech clusters of more recent origin in the US and a limited number of regions in other countries. In general, the success stories appear difficult to replicate. Nonetheless, OECD work on territorial policy and reviews of regions shows that cluster development is an ambition in economic development policy in a large proportion of OECD regions, including intermediate and rural regions, where it is seen as a relatively low-cost reorientation for enterprise policy. The series of territorial reviews illustrate the many different varieties of clusters that are found across the OECD, and the difficulty that policy makers face in designing effective policies in such diverse contexts. Nevertheless, while the enterprise systems found in most OECD regions diverge sharply from the Northern Italy/Silicon Valley models, many of the same competitive advantages accrue – a similar potential for positive feedbacks and linkages exist. In Montreal and Helsinki, for example, where the respective clusters on which each metropolitan economy is strongly based (aerospace, biotechnology and ICT in Montreal and ICT in Helsinki) have characteristics that do not fit neatly into the industrial cluster model – for example, large multinationals tend to dominate the clusters in each city. Nonetheless, a form of cluster development policy is likely to be the cornerstone of the regional competitiveness policy in each place: for example, the emphasis for Montreal is on building relational assets among local actors in both existing and emerging clusters. A better understanding of how classic "cluster" principles can be used to inform policy for a wider set of regional economic contexts – the large majority of cases – where cluster conditions are only partially present, is an important area for further research.

At the same time, the mechanisms at work within most enterprise systems are poorly understood or are sufficiently intangible to be difficult for policy interventions to reach. For example, two key "unknowns" are 1) the channels for information exchange and co-operation that firms, particularly SMEs, actually use and 2) the current gaps – communicative, cultural, management style – among firms and between firms and other participants in the regional economy, particularly government and non-government producers/diffusers of knowledge and technology. Services for clusters depend on there being a clear sense of the added value of joint working, which is often lacking.

More than most areas of regional policy, there is an obvious need for evaluation of the outcomes from these policies. But, impact evaluation of cluster policies poses numerous problems. In essence, the more rigorous the conceptual definition, the more difficult it is to measure. In other words, if the outcomes are measured simply in terms of co-location of enterprises, services received or meetings arranged, then the measurement can be relatively sound. However, when the definition of positive clustering outcomes is based on "levels of informal collaboration" or on the presence of "informal knowledge spillovers" then assessing the contribution of policy to changes in firm productivity becomes qualitative (Martin and Sunley, 2003). Moreover, cluster policies have been applied in very different regional contexts and with differing levels of funding.[6] As a result, despite the enormous interest, cluster policies still have much to prove in terms of their effectiveness and general applicability.

Linking education, research and business

Until recently, universities were viewed in most member countries as essentially providers of basic knowledge for the labour market, and most remain relatively isolated from the rest of the economy. This situation is, however, changing. Pressures to enhance the employability of university graduates brought workplace skill issues onto the tertiary education agenda. Moreover, innovation based competition has increased the demand for access to university expertise and research findings. As a consequence, higher education institutions are now called upon for tasks that go far beyond their traditional teaching and research functions, such as regional engagement, urban planning, and, perhaps most significantly, collaboration with firms.

In practice: an increasingly important focus for regional development policies

Beyond their traditional functions in research and teaching, many higher education institutions (HEI) have now taken steps to respond better to the needs of their regions and to transform themselves into entrepreneurial universities. The table outlines the main ways in which higher education institutions interact with their local environments (Lawton Smith, 2005).

Table 1.1. **Taxonomy of kinds of relationships between tertiary education and business**

Innovation	
Knowledge production and transfer of knowledge	Formal research collaboration
	Links to global technological and scientific networks
	Take up of patents and licences
	Published papers – *e.g.* joint academic industry articles
	Contract research
	Specialisation in new technologies and leadership of new industries
Technological applications of research, expertise and in-house facilities	Testing services *e.g.* carbon dating, equipment testing
	prospects of application (*e.g.* X-rays, lasers).
	Engineering design tools and techniques – including modelling, simulation and theoretical prediction
	Product and process development
	Instrumentation
SME support	Prototype development,
	Consultancy services
	testing
	Contract research
Entrepreneurial culture, entrepreneurship and cluster development	
Entrepreneurship	Spin-offs
Buildings	Science parks
	Incubators
	Cluster focused technical assistance
Networks	Network facilitators, developing academic and non-academic networks
	Mentoring services
Image	Place marketing and development, promoting brand image, organisation of showcase events
Human capital	
Recruitment	Recruitment of graduated undergraduate and post-grad students
Training	Vocational courses – technical and teaching *e.g.* technicians training
Vocational	Placement schemes
Public access to knowledge	Continuing professional development and extension programmes
	Public lectures and public access to libraries, museums, galleries, sporting facilities
Direct multiplier effects	
	Staff, student and visitor spending
	Purchase of goods and services
	Contribution to tourism
	Support for inward investment
Governance	
Engagement in decision-making processes	Economic
	Cultural
	Sustainability
	Transport
Contribution to sustainable development	Contribution to the quality of the built environment
	Contribution to property-led urban regeneration
	Provision of student accommodation
	Effects on parking and traffic problems
	Other land use issues

Source: Patel 2002, Glasson 2003, survey by Helen Lawton Smith.

With respect to links with enterprises, although the degree varies greatly by region and by country, interactions with business have generally increased. A recent OECD report described the different rationales and mechanisms according to the types of firms involved and often on the technological fields represented. Three main types of relationship are distinguished:

- Relations between multinational enterprises and world-class universities. Multinational enterprises are externalising part of their research and development activities and are looking for the best laboratories, scientists and students.
- Relations between universities and small high-technology firms (spin-offs and knowledge intensive business services).
- Relations developing in a regional context between firms (often SMEs) and the local university. Here firms are looking for short-term, problem-solving capabilities.

These new roles for universities are particularly visible in the US. For example, many public research universities have long-established missions to encourage business development. With respect to the key elements in university-business links, a recent study of the most successful US universities highlighted the importance of university leadership (in championing economic development and innovation missions), faculty culture and rewards, active and well-organized technology transfer and entrepreneurship incentives throughout the university, and strong partnerships with private and other public organisations (see Box 1.7) (Tornatzky et al., 2002).

One of the best known models of linkages between universities and companies is the MIT Industrial Liaison Programme. After paying a membership fee that varies according to their size, companies have unlimited access to specialised information services and seminar series, a monthly newsletter that includes details of ongoing research and outlines new inventions, the directory of MIT research activity organised by area of expertise to make it easier to track specific interests, faculty visits and expert meetings for companies that often result in consultancy or research sponsorship. The programme is particularly attractive to companies because it is managed by a panel of Industrial Liaison Officers (ILO), each responsible for a focused portfolio of companies with the responsibility to serve their unique interests and needs.

In many other OECD countries, a similar pattern is now emerging. In Sweden, for example, universities have been given the formal mission (in 1996) of promoting regional innovation. In several locations in Sweden, universities have been active in forming new academic-business linkages, establishing regional technology partnerships, and offering new kinds of entrepreneurial training (Cooke, 2004). The Öresund region provides a good

> Box 1.7. **Research-industry relationships: the example of Georgia Tech**
>
> The top-ranked "Innovation-U" in a recent study by the Southern Growth Policies Board was Georgia Institute of Technology (Georgia Tech) in Atlanta. A prominent research university, Georgia Tech also works closely with Georgia state government, local communities, and businesses in a variety of technology-focused initiatives. Economic development and technology transfer activities are housed in Georgia Tech's Economic Development Institute, which operates a network of regional technology transfer offices in 18 communities in the state, and in its parent organisation, the Office of Economic Development and Technology Ventures, which sponsors advanced technology incubators and faculty commercialization programs. Many other academic units, research centres, and the university's continuing education program support regional innovation missions. Long-term results from Georgia Tech's regional innovation efforts include a massive expansion of industry-research partnerships, the development of cutting-edge technology-based economic development programs, scores of new high technology start-ups, ongoing technology and business support for thousands of existing firms, specialized industry training of thousands of people each year, and the fostering of systems for entrepreneurial development in the state.
>
> Other "Innovation-U's" highly ranked in the study were Carnegie-Mellon, North Carolina State, Ohio State, Pennsylvania State, Purdue, Stanford, Texas A&M, UC San Diego, Utah, Wisconsin, and Virginia Tech. The practices and partnerships of these innovative universities emerge from the "grass roots" – and not from the federal government or through a top-down standardized formula. "There are common practices," the study authors conclude, "but no one model or approach is followed by all" (Tornatzky et al., 2002).*
>
> * See also OECD, *Benchmarking of Science Industry Relationships*, 2002.
> Source: Quoted in *OECD Territorial Reviews* of Japan (2005).

illustration of these collaborative initiatives, with the added twist of being a cross-border network covering both Sweden and Denmark (see Box 1.8).

However, elsewhere in the OECD the role of universities in regional development is at an early stage. The third CEC Community Innovation Survey[7] (2004) shows that only 5% of innovating firms indicated that universities were highly important for innovation (3% for government or private non-profit research institutes) compared with 28% from clients or customers (the highest external source) (Lawton Smith 2005). Cooke *et al.* (2002) in their study of Tel Aviv, Belfast and Cardiff, like numerous other studies of larger cities like London and Amsterdam, have found that

Box 1.8. **Higher education and industrial clusters in the Öresund region**

The Öresund is a cross-border region comprising the Danish island of Zealand including Copenhagen the capital city and the Skåne region, with Malmö, Sweden's second largest city. Since 2000, the two cities have been linked by a rail and road bridge. This new transport infrastructure has resulted in a single functional region spanning two different countries. The Öresund region has developed significant strength in knowledge – intensive activities including the medical and pharmaceutical industries and certain segments of information and communication technology industries. It is also strong in food processing and has developed an environmental cluster with companies that either produce environmental technologies or make production, products and services more environment friendly.

The education sector seems to be in the forefront of promoting co-operation among knowledge generators and users. With a total of 20 universities with 130 000 students, the Öresund Region has many strengths in the education and research sector. More important than simply the existence of these resources, however, is the co-operation between universities that has developed over time.* Long-term informal co-operation was formalised in 1997 with the creation of the Öresund University. This institution has been a leading actor not only around formal scientific research and education (i.e. Öresund Science Region), but also around the creation of institutions to promote more informal networking activity and information sharing for economic activities. Working in collaboration with researchers, business leaders and policy makers throughout the region, the Öresund University has helped in identifying critical driving growth clusters and facilitating the development of networking associations in each of those clusters. These organisations – Medicon Valley Academy, Öresund IT Academy, Öresund Food Network, and Öresund Environment – are already playing an important role in promoting networking and integration across the region, and show a great deal of promise for the future.

Medicon Valley Academy (MVA) started out as a publicly funded initiative, set up in 1997 as a regional and bi-national network organisation. In 2000, it went through a significant re-organisation to become a membership-based organisation, funded primarily by membership fees (that accounted for 67% of total funding for the year, with conference fees providing another 17%). The aim is to support a regional biotech forum for debate and networking. The Academy has also organised a series of ongoing sub-groups promoting networking around topics, such as human resources in bio-tech, bio-molecular structures and dynamics, cancer research and health economics. A PhD programme involving 12 students is part of the MVA and aim at strengthening co-operation between public institutions and private companies about product development. While catalysed by the Öresund University and significant public sector funding, the organisation has now developed a dynamic of its own and plays an active role in promoting information sharing and knowledge development in the region.

* One interesting evidence of this is the early efforts to develop a commonly administered "Öresund Summer University" for international students, who take courses at different institutions in the region. Currently, co-operation in education and research affect many aspects of the activities of universities. Still, utilisation of resources could be intensified, including such areas as courses offered, library collections, laboratories and other facilities, which can be made readily accessible to students and researchers throughout the region.

Source: OECD Territorial Review of Öresund (2002).

universities often have much stronger innovation interactions with businesses at national and international levels (Lawton Smith 2005).

The influence of regulation

Universities are traditionally managed and supervised by ministries of education and ministries of research (when these competencies are separated) at national or, in federal and decentralised countries, at regional level. Their strategic missions are influenced by the programmes, instructions (in the case of public universities) and regulations designed by the ministries. Moreover, regulatory frameworks can also reduce the freedom and incentives for institutions and individual researchers to engage in projects with the private sector. OECD countries have introduced reforms in the governance of universities with the aim of increasing their flexibility and autonomy and, thereby, promoting better interaction among universities, public research organisations and firms. Japan is a good example (see Box 1.9). The emphasis

---

Box 1.9. Deregulation of universities: the case of Japan

In 2004, Japan's national universities – positioned as part of the central government for more than a century – were reformed as independent public corporations. University faculty members are now non-governmental employees, not civil servants as before. From 2004 onwards, it will also be possible for other public universities to be incorporated according to the judgement of the prefectural government concerned. Selective university mergers to create economies of scale and other changes in academic incentive and evaluation systems are also under way. Universities are also rapidly establishing Technology Licensing Offices, incubators, collaborative industry-research centres, and other programmes to promote research commercialisation and regional development.* The aim is to stimulate a more flexible, competitive and entrepreneurial university system in Japan that can not only undertake world-class research but also have significant impacts on regional innovation and development. Whether the latter goal is achieved will depend not only on the extent to which universities themselves embrace these reforms, but also on the ways in which regions and localities can build new linkages between universities, economic sectors, and territorial innovation strategies.

* The 1999 Industry Revitalization Law (also known as the "Japanese Bayh-Dole Act") reduced obstacles to collaboration between universities and private enterprises and also allowed private firms to acquire intellectual property rights from publicly-funded research. This has given stimulus to the growth of Technology Transfer Offices in Japan, of which there are now 37. See also: J. Rissanen and J. Viitanen, *Report on Japanese Technology Licensing Offices and R&D Intellectual Property Right Issues*, The Finnish Institute in Japan, 2001.

Source: OECD (2005), *Territorial Review* of Japan.

of the government, apparent for a number of years, is to ensure that this research and technical expertise are translated into commercial success for Japanese firms. However, until recently there were strong disincentives for employees of universities to work on joint projects with companies. This is now changing.

Mismatch between offer and demand

In some cases, it is the local enterprises themselves that are reticent. Small firms are often reluctant to engage in joint activities with universities, either because they are unable to precisely formalise their research and expertise needs, or because they lack information about the supply of university research findings and services and consider them to be too basic or abstract. Thus, the explanation for limited engagement between research institutions and business can be a result of a simple mis-match between what the university can offer and what firms expect. For example, although regional universities in Korea have already started to take useful steps in that direction,[8] they need to improve the quality of their R&D and re-balance their teaching, research and regional economic engagement functions. According to a survey by Busan University, only 7.3% of firms pick innovative ideas from local universities. Even the few efforts from large firms such as Renault-Samsung Motors to join in co-operative research initiatives with local universities have been aborted because the level of research in the universities was not attractive enough to firms. Both the national and regional governments in Korea will be investing heavily to up-grade the capacity of regional universities in order to reduce this gap (OECD 2005).

Table 1.2. **Source of innovative ideas for Busan firms**
% of 1 000 firms

Source of innovative ideas	Yes	No
Universities	7.3	92.7
Government-funded research institutes	4.2	95.8
Public laboratories	3.8	96.2
Societies and leagues	5.3	94.7
Research unions	2.8	97.2
Private research institutes	3.3	96.7

Source: Asian Institute for Regional Innovation, December 2003.

Small business expectations and technological needs clearly differ significantly from those of large firms. Such firms are, nevertheless, increasingly pressed to adopt cutting edge technologies both for their own production and when they are part of a supply chain and linked with large customers. Technology intermediaries or technology "clinics" (such as those in Finland) can help to link SMEs and knowledge institutions. These initiatives provide brokerage services and put firms in contact with university experts who may be able to provide them with solutions to their problem.

Links with other innovation policies: a key factor in both technopole and cluster initiatives

In practice, many initiatives combine links between research and business with elements of the technology centre and clusters policies discussed above. If the technopole is well designed and funded, then there is a better chance that the linkages between the education/research side and the enterprises located on site will develop. The comprehensive policy of Centres of Expertise in Finland is a good example (see Box 1.10).

> **Box 1.10. Centres of Expertise, Finland**
>
> The Centre of Expertise (CoE) action programme began in 1994 and was initially programmed to last five years until 1999. It was so successful that the Finnish Government decided to embark on a new eight-year programme spanning the period 1999 to 2006. The first programme sought to complement national policy for innovation by pooling regional and national resources to develop specific industry sectors (mainly traditional high-tech) into selected, internationally competitive fields of expertise. More specifically, it aimed to forge innovation and creativity among small and medium-sized companies by encouraging them to co-operate with training institutes, universities, and research centres in and around a region. The long-term objective was to enhance regional competitiveness and to increase the number of high-tech products, companies, and jobs.
>
> The guiding principle of the programme is that it is open to competition, which is why only the very best units receive a national CoE status. To participate in the programme, the units must demonstrate an internationally high-level concentration of expertise, effectiveness, innovation, and efficient organisation. CoEs also compete annually for government funding. This basic funding is matched by a contribution from the region's local partners. So far, relatively small amounts of state subsidies have helped generate significant economic growth within the selected fields of expertise. For the first programme, however, the most important source of funding was the private sector (27%). Next came the National Technology Agency (TEKES), accounting for 25 %, and cities, municipalities and regional councils, all together accounting for 24 % of funding. Meanwhile, the EU contributed to 17 % of total project costs.

> **Box 1.10. Centres of Expertise, Finland** *(cont.)*
>
> The first CoE programme exceeded all expectations and had a hugely positive impact on job creation and entrepreneurial activity.[1] To give an idea of the scale of its success, the number of regional CoEs has risen from 8 to 22 since the programme started. The CoE projects have not only generated a new economic activity, but have also (by utilising research and the special expertise specific to the regions) furthered business development and new contacts and promoted new industries. By 2004, there were over 1 750 regional projects underway at the centres, and the programme had contributed to the creation of well over 10 000 new jobs and has safeguarded 18 000 existing ones. About 850 new enterprises in the fields concerned were established during the first years of the programme. With better co-ordination of the CoE operations nation-wide, there has been increasing collaboration between centres, leading to more advanced innovations, often of international significance. The Pro Electronica international development project in Oulu is an example of this.[2]
>
> The expanded programme, inspired by the results of the first, has been reoriented and expanded. Its four main goals are to identify regional strengths and create economic growth; increase the number of competitive products, services, enterprises, and jobs based on the highest standard of expertise; attract international investment and leading experts; and continually reinforce and regenerate regional expertise. In particular, the concept of the field of expertise has been broadened from the traditional high-tech sectors to include new fields, such as new media, the cultural business, the recreational experience industry, design, quality and environmental expertise. This reorientation ensures that the Centres of Expertise of the future will represent increasingly attractive targets for international private and corporate investment.
>
> 1. Urban Exchange Initiative III: Urban development through expertise, research and information (Informal Meeting of the Ministers responsible for Spatial Planning and Urban/Regional Policy of the European Union at Tampere, October 1999). Participants included the Ministry of the Interior, Finland, in co-operation with several experts in Finland and other EU member states.
> 2. See: *www.intermin.fi/suom/oske/en/osket/oulu.html*.
>
> *Source: OECD Territorial Review of Finland* (forthcoming).

The emerging role of technical colleges

As part of the policy effort to improve interaction within regional innovation systems, particularly with respect to SMEs, technical colleges have been increasingly recognised as having a key role to play, especially in peripheral and less-favoured regions. These organisations are variously called community colleges (Canada, USA), technical colleges (Denmark, USA, and

UK), further education colleges (UK), technical and further education institutions (Australia), polytechnics or *Fachhochschulen* (Austria, Belgium, Germany, the Netherlands, New Zealand) and institutes of technology (Finland, Ireland). However, they have in common a role as upper secondary or tertiary education, targeting occupations such as technicians and engineers, and having a strong regional or local focus in their operations (OECD 1999).

Technical colleges are unusual and even unique among public educational institutions in the explicitness and intensity with which their economic aims complement their educational goals. A large proportion of technical college systems were formulated or have been reformulated to serve both the student bodies and regional economies. This economic value of technical colleges is based on an inherent flexibility that allows them to respond quickly to the demands of the workplace caused by growth, technology, and/or economic readjustment. Over time, the most entrepreneurial and innovative of the colleges have used their resources and expertise not only to react to technological change but to influence rates of technology adoption.

Technical colleges are generally acknowledged as vital ingredients in regional technology and innovation strategies – retraining in the wake of technological change and ensuring a sufficient flow of technically proficient workers into the region to meet needs and allow for growth. Most colleges now include some dimensions of technology development within their core missions. Just how far a college is willing to extend its reach beyond its traditional student client base towards a newer and less conventional business client base depends on a number of factors, *i.e.*, college and business leadership, national and state policies and regulations, budgets, alternative sources of technology training and assistance, degree of flexibility and autonomy, and entrepreneurial energy. The role of technical colleges, as described above, seems appropriate for all types of regions, although their size and specialisation will differ from case to case. Technical colleges have the ability to specialise in all types of productive activities, even those based on natural endowments like mineral exploitation or tourism. They already respond to the mass need for human capital formation and thus their contribution to regional developments comes as a result of broadening their scope. In that sense additional investment is lower than in the two cases discussed previously. In high-tech regions they are expected to specialise in high-tech sectors, in industrial districts they would need to offer technology services in the already existing clusters, whereas in underdeveloped regions they would limit their activities to the organisational and technology transfer needs of the local productive activities.

> Box 1.11. **HES in Switzerland**
>
> The Swiss HES (Colleges of Higher Education) programme is a major initiative in the field of education, innovation and regional development. It should help in bridging the gap between the high level of research in the country and the more modest level of innovation performance. HESs are training highly qualified professionals by offering a combination of practical and theoretical education within the framework of a short-term degree programme. Further, HESs are also promoting applied research and technology transfer to SMEs. The specialisation of these could have many potential economic applications; and if a certain level of quality of research and private R&D is obtained, continuing experimentation can ensure that specialised knowledge will evolve constantly and be applied in new ways. Further, public investments in specialised HES may be extremely cost efficient if local industrialists become involved and the HES succeed in spurring private investments in training and R&D. Thus, a great political effort should be devoted not just to the specialisation of the HES, but also to ensuring that local industrialists participate in the process. Further, HES could function as local technology service providers. In co-operation with local authorities, some HES could even take on the role of industrial development councils, arranging seminars and informal meetings about, for example, best technological practices, or new international, federal, and cantonal industry regulations. Such meetings also have a great potential for developing local networking cultures.
>
> *Source: OECD Territorial Review of Switzerland.*

3. Competitive regions: policies for the wider business environment

As discussed above, innovation and knowledge have emerged as the principal targets for regional policies. In order to be cost-effective and have regional impact in all types of region, these knowledge-based policies need to be complemented with other measures. These other measures should aim to improve the "enabling environment" of the specific region that supports business activity. The common denominator in current thinking is an emphasis on place-specific externalities based on better exploiting unused potential and assets. Many of the targets of these policies were formerly more closely associated with social or environmental policies, but are now considered from the perspective of their impact on economic performance. Policy instruments tend to focus on providing collective goods that improve what has been termed the "quality of place" – the attractiveness and functioning of the region as a whole, that improve its accessibility, and so on. Without a supportive environment, cluster development, regional innovation strategies and so on will not have a significant impact on performance. Worse, they could even lead policy back towards artificially supporting private sector development without addressing key market failures first. In terms of specific policies, OECD work has focused on two main groups of policies that exemplify the issue of providing public, collective goods for economic development in the framework of regional competitiveness:

- investing in the "enabling" environment; and
- focusing development on under-used natural, cultural and historical amenities.

Investing in the "enabling" environment

As discussed earlier, the regional environment in which firms are located plays an important role in influencing their productivity, both directly with respect to the level of services and infrastructure that are available and indirectly, for example through the ability of the region to offer quality of life advantages for workers. The regional environment includes a range of factors that either encourage or inhibit business activity – the quality of transport and communications infrastructure, local tax rates and the return in terms of efficient public service provision, the availability of land and housing, including affordable housing, the standard of the education system at all levels, and so on. This is strongly linked to the strategic management of the territory and the level and allocation of investment that national and local authorities jointly provide. Attention tends to focus on the framework conditions for business, the tangible factors that increase or decrease production costs – local tax regimes, transport and so on.

OECD work across a range of different region-types demonstrates that the presence of efficient physical infrastructure and related services remains a key to economic development. The expectation that improvements in physical infrastructure will generate productivity gains for local businesses and increase the attractiveness of an area for investment has been a recurring theme in OECD reviews of specific regions. High quality infrastructure and services are accepted as being vital to a strong economy – locally, regionally and nationally. Taking the example of transport, upgrading infrastructure changes access (travel times) which affects property prices and economic rents, influences decisions of households (residential location, patterns of consumption) and firms (production location, access to markets and investment decisions) and these, in turn, should have a net positive impact on the economy, increase tax revenues, create employment and generate resources for further investment. For business, the benefits could include:

- access to a wider labour market pool, with more diverse competencies;
- faster access to suppliers and customers, which reduces transaction costs;

I. STRATEGIES

- expanded market reach (including choice of suppliers, as well as expanded customer base);
- reduction of land use constraints.

Figure 1.1. **Transport infrastructure investment and economic growth effects**

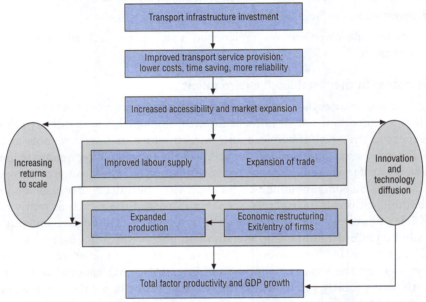

Source: OECD (2003) "Decoupling transport demand and economic growth"; adapted from Larkshmanan, 2002.

Although there are issues of regional impact measurement and diminishing returns from upgrading of infrastructure to consider, transport improvement is generally seen as generating strong positive externalities and more efficient allocation of resources throughout the local economy. From a policy perspective, the assumption of a multiplier effect from investment is appealing. In an attempt to link given levels of transport infrastructure expenditure with productivity gain and employment growth, the European Commission has produced estimates of potentially substantial output/employment gains from the TransEuropeanNetwork (TEN) programme. Increases of 0.25% in EU GDP and in employment of 0.11% are predicted as a result of the priority TEN projects between 2005 and 2025, with the employment creation potential of the full network estimated at 800 000 jobs. An OECD review of regional policy in the Czech Republic (OECD, 2004) strongly emphasises the importance of adequate domestic and international road and rail connections. For example, it highlights the accessibility issues for Ostrava, third city in the country, which is still not connected to the rest of the highway network, thus stifling the development efforts of an industrial area undergoing deep restructuring and experiencing high unemployment. Poor accessibility prevents Ostrava, and more generally the region of Moravia-Silesia from attracting a more sizeable share of FDI in spite of its assets (human capital, excellent university and research centres) and strong financial and other incentives for investors.

Even if the costs and benefits of infrastructure investment are difficult to measure precisely, from the perspective of most policymakers this type of forecast ensures that strategies for competitiveness include a strong focus on upgrading infrastructure and delivering better quality transport services.

Case studies suggest, however, that the construction or upgrading of transportation infrastructure can undoubtedly have a fundamental influence on a region's economic development, but economic growth is not automatic. Growth effects are likely to appear when positive externalities exist in the region. The discussion of innovation and specialisation suggests that both depend on an efficient, sufficient infrastructure network in order for the different types of spatial agglomeration effects to operate. Faster transport connections can potentially incite positive externalities that exist in various markets – typically unexhausted economies of scale, scope, agglomeration, density or network – and consequently improve (labour) productivity, enhance output, reduce production costs and promote more efficient use of resources. If latent economies do not exist, improvements in accessibility could lead to changes in existing transport flows and spatial patterns without having long-term effects on growth. The OECD review of the Öresund region is clear that the bridge between Copenhagen and Malmö is only one element in a wider strategy to build on the complementarities that have developed between the two regional economies (see Box 1.12). The challenge for policymakers explicit in the recommendations is to ensure that the potential in the now unified labour market, research community, and enterprise systems is realised. Vienna-Bratislava provides a similar example: it is expected that accession of Slovakia to the EU will allow a larger and stronger functional economic area to develop that generates scale and scope advantages for local firms that did not exist before. Providing infrastructure to link the opened border is a first step, but then policy challenges relating to economic specialisation, innovation and governance come to the fore (see also Box 2.8).

At the same time, constraints on infrastructure development are growing. In particular, the cost of developing new infrastructure has increased dramatically, while maintenance represents a significant share of total infrastructure spending in OECD countries. In Japan, for example, projections regarding the proportion of total investment that will need to be spent on maintenance suggest that in the relatively near term, expenditures on renewal of infrastructure will equal expenditures on new facilities. Assuming

Box 1.12. **Impacts of the Öresund bridge on attractiveness and competitiveness**

Three territorial levels of impact should be considered: the regional level, the national level and the international level. At each level, the effects are different and more importantly, the reactions of stakeholders are quite diverse.

At the regional level (Öresund), the new infrastructural links – in addition to the Bridge – have framed a new internal network of mobility and communication which has increased interactions among people, firms and institutions. The intensified interactions increase the "value" of internal interdependence as a factor of robustness of the local economy and society in terms of competitiveness and attractiveness. The main feature of this evaluation is identifiable in the strengthening of the two main poles, Copenhagen and Malmö, but that growth has also affected a multiplicity of areas within the region. Thus, on both sides of the Strait, the spatial "continuity" between cores and hinterlands causes fewer problems today than in the past.

The competitive role of the Öresund Region is also modifying its relative position within the two countries. This is a relatively minor problem for Denmark, where Copenhagen's leading role increased as a national capital and as a main attraction pole in the Öresund Region. On the contrary in Sweden, the growth of the Öresund Region will inevitably create a more significant impact. In particular, Stockholm and Gothenburg have perceived the importance of the Öresund growth and are reacting to its increased competitiveness. On one side, the reinforcement of Malmö and Skåne has caused a new development area in Sweden, speeding up the overall country output. On the other side, the acceleration of growth in Southern Sweden has upset the traditional political agreement on regional policy in the country. In fact, due to its marginality, the North had always been strongly privileged in the allocation of "regional" subsidies, as the central part of Sweden (along the Stockholm-Gothenburg axis) was self-sufficient and the South, despite the industrial decline in Malmö, had always been considered already "developed" and was not considered worthy of particular intervention. The opportunity represented by the growth of the Öresund Region has modified this attitude. The political orientation towards favouring equality rather than supporting dynamism is slowly reversing and a greater attention is being paid to the Southern part of Sweden, also because it has become a stronger link toward the rest of Europe.

The third territorial level of competitiveness, which is indirectly enhanced by the new infrastructural investments in the Öresund Region, takes place on an international scale. The fact that Copenhagen and Malmö are starting to be considered a joint global hub and have climbed in the European hierarchy of metropolitan areas is indeed playing a significant role in the competitive growth of the region. The most meaningful factor of such increase in competitiveness is the international integration process. Comparable experiences are the Channel Tunnel between France and Great Britain, and the new highway system planned between Vienna, Prague and Budapest.

Source: OECD Territorial Review of Öresund.

limited increases in total spending, Japan's maintenance budget is likely to overtake the budget for new construction in the next decade (OECD, 2005). In consequence, infrastructure investment policies in the OECD tend to emphasise three aspects: 1) better use of existing infrastructure, 2) better targeting of new investment and 3) mechanisms to increase the level of private sector financing in public projects.

In this context, communications infrastructure promises both substantial returns on targeted investment and important leveraging possibilities. Communications infrastructure produces generalisable time-savings for most economic sectors that can translate into economic growth and employment creation potential. Rural policy in particular is focusing on how enterprises and entrepreneurs in peripheral regions can use advanced communications networks to gain access to markets located in core regions. A review of policies to promote ICT in rural areas identified three categories of economic activity: tele-business (call centres and business process out-sourcing), tele-work, and start ups focusing on multimedia and software design, often linked to providing services (marketing, etc.) for both local customers (*e.g.* local businesses, local governments, etc.) and those further afield. There is a close link between the increased use of ICT in rural locations and growing interest among policymakers in rural enterprise creation, including how cluster policies can be adapted from their general targets which are urban or intermediate regions to be relevant for rural regions as well.

Focusing development on under-used natural, cultural and historical amenities

Amenities as a core of rural development policy

There is increasing recognition that "quality of place" has an important influence on regional competitiveness, particularly with respect to attracting and retaining mobile resources such as investment and skilled labour. This emphasis on environmental quality and attractiveness can be seen in ongoing OECD work in fields such as the attractiveness of cities, sustainable use of housing and building stock, among others. Regional development policies in both rural and urban areas are increasingly looking to harness the potential of their "amenities", the varied natural and man-made attractions that differentiate one region from another and that provide the "raw material" for different kinds of economic activities ranging from tourism and entertainment industries to speciality products and foods.

These diverse amenities have some shared characteristics that mean that they are often not effectively provided through conventional markets. Amenities often exhibit what are termed public good characteristics, specifically, they are to some extent *non-rival* and *non-excludable*:

Box 1.13. **Some examples of rural amenities assessed by OECD**

Australia: Native forests are one of Australia's premier suppliers of rural amenities. However, tensions have been increasing between the need to conserve these forests for environmental and recreational purposes, on one hand, and support for traditional forest industries, on the other hand. The Regional Forest Agreement (RFA) process, on which the case study focuses, is designed to reduce these conflicts and promote a multifunctional forest system by setting a framework (in the form of a signed agreement) for forest resource planning over twenty years.

Austria: Alpine pasture makes up 20 per cent of all land in Austria. How it is managed has important implications for landscape, tourism and prevention of natural disasters. In addition to its productive function, mountain farming maintains sensitive alpine eco-systems and cultural landscapes. In 1972, the Mountain Farmers Special Programme was set up to maintain the multiple functions of mountain agriculture as well as economic and social stability. Under the programme, mountain farmers receive government payments based on their level of "difficulty" (as related to transportation constraints and small size).

France: Established in 1967, France's Regional Nature Parks (RNP) are intended to implement development schemes based on conservation, management, and valorisation of natural and man-made amenities. They are located only in areas with natural and cultural heritage of outstanding quality. The overall objective is to reconcile the preservation of these amenities with the area's economic development. There are now 32 such regional nature parks in France, covering nearly 10 per cent of the country and involving over 2 600 rural communes.

Japan: Tanadas are stair-shaped rice fields or terraces built on steep mountain slopes. They were developed in ancient Japan and used in nearly all regions of the country. Today, there are about 220 000 hectares of *Tanadas* on slopes exceeding 1/20. They account for about eight per cent of all land planted in rice. *Tanadas* are appreciated not only for their scenic appearance, but also because they represent accumulated tradition, culture, and local identity. However, the laborious work required for their maintenance is causing them to disappear rapidly. Several measures to reverse the decline are being taken, particularly by local governments. The Temporary Owner System, for example, is intended to market amenity value by inviting city-dwellers to work the terraced fields as if they were owners of *Tanadas*. They typically assist farmers on several weekends during the busiest seasons. Another example is the *Tanada* fund, which subsidises farmers to continue to farm the traditional, terraced fields.

> Box 1.13. **Some examples of rural amenities assessed by OECD** *(cont.)*
>
> **Switzerland:** The border trail Napfbergland follows one of the country's most distinctive economic, ethnic, and cultural dividing lines: a border between two cantons, one western and one central European culture, one Protestant and one Catholic faith. The Napf border area has not only a unique cultural identity but also a scenic, pre-Alpine landscape comprised of forested areas, historic sites, and traditionally cultivated small farms. The area's individual attractions are not considered as spectacular as those in the more mountainous Alpine region. However, as a series of natural and cultural sites connected by the border, they are a valuable asset. Hence, the trail project was begun in 1997 with government support to diversity the economy through tourism. By creating a critical mass of attractions, project leaders hope to attract visitors and market labelled products from the border trail region.

- *non-rival* in that the availability of the good for consumption by one person is not decreased by consumption by another (except where over-use has negative impacts on the quality of the amenity). A typical example here would be an attractive landscape. Public access to the countryside can be enjoyed by substantial numbers of people without affecting each others' enjoyment, but at some point congestion arises such that the quality of the recreation experience is reduced;
- *non-excludable* in that once provided, it is often impractical to exclude people from enjoying their consumption. Landscape can in principle be rendered excludable by setting up and enforcing boundaries around an area, but in practice the cost of so doing would exceed the revenue that might be obtained from the undertaking.

These public good characteristics mean that there are few direct incentives for private actors, or even public actors, to provide, maintain or invest in the supply of amenities because it is difficult to convert this investment into revenue accruing solely or in large part to the investors. Nonetheless, these are clearly important assets for a region and can represent an important, sometimes the only, source of competitive advantage in some rural regions. Moreover, the valorisation of amenities is often the best incentive for their conservation. The central question is: how can policymakers "internalise" the externality benefits inherent in rural amenities so that providers have financial incentives to maintain and/or provide access to these amenities at a reasonable cost to the different "users" (both individual visitors and, in many cases, society as a whole). Two key elements in this process are 1) estimating the value of (demand for) amenities and thereby setting prices, and 2) encouraging the creation of market or market-type mechanisms to transfer benefits.

Work on valuing amenities has its origins in efforts to quantify the multifunctional dimension of agriculture by separating amenity provision from commodity production functions, as well as in attempts to estimate the value of biodiversity and other ecological assets.[9] Recreational (use) value of rural amenities can be estimated using revealed (observed, actual) preference models that are relatively robust. However, the non-use values of rural amenities expressed as, for example, willingness-to-pay to preserve biodiversity or agricultural landscapes have to be based on stated preference techniques, and are thus more problematic. As such, the ability of policymakers to estimate the cost effectiveness of programmes that support amenities with significant non-use values is limited, which partly explains why policies to develop markets or substitute markets for amenity goods are preferred.[10]

Instruments to ensure optimal provision of amenities can take several different forms: for example, creating direct amenity markets (paying for access, user fees); creating amenity-related commodity markets ("green" markets); buying of resources by interest groups; incentives, taxes and subsidies to providers; etc. There are two principal types of policy that include market-oriented economic instruments: 1) policies to stimulate co-ordination between supply and demand, and 2) instruments that provide regulatory or financial incentives or disincentives to act in a particular way.

1) *Policies designed to stimulate direct co-ordination between amenity providers and beneficiaries,* either through the market or through co-operation among agents acting collectively.

- *Support for enhancement of the commercial value of amenities:* The aim is to encourage commercial transactions between providers and beneficiaries of amenities with regard to either the amenities themselves or to related products. Targeted amenities are those which are potentially private goods so that the establishment of an amenity market is possible with certain assistance, such as the introduction of a institutional framework for amenity markets, supports for the valorisation by rural enterprises, official certification on amenity value added products, etc.

- *Support for collective action:* The aim is to promote and support actions initiated and pursued by groups of agents with a view to adjusting amenity supply and demand. Targeted amenities are those which need collective action for their maintenance and/or valorisation by providers and beneficiaries.

Table 1.3. **Types of collective action for mise en valeur of amenities**

Type of action	Action and aims
Collective action by amenity providers	1. Networking among complementary amenities: to make amenities more visible and so open up more possibilities for their valorisation. 2. Networking for the certification of several amenity offerings: to enable commercial valorisation by certifying collectively the link between product and amenity. 3. Self-regulation by voluntary agreement among providers: to supply an amenity jointly and so preserve possibilities for its valorisation.
Collective action by beneficiaries	4. Pooling and communication of private demand: to communicate a social demand to providers and the authorities. 5. Direct action on provision of an amenity: to purchase lands of amenities or certain rights to preserve them.
Concerted action by providers and beneficiaries	6. Negotiation with a view to voluntary agreement between supply and demand sides: to communicate supply and demand and agree how to share the burden for optimum provision. 7. Concerted territorial management of amenities: to provide an appropriate territorial scale to achieve optimum valorisation of amenities.

2) Policies designed to change the economic ground rules so as to guide individual acts in a given direction. Under this heading come economic incentives or regulations that make it worthwhile to adopt practices favourable to amenity provision. In these cases the authorities try to "control" amenity supply themselves. Targeted amenities are mainly those which are public goods and/ or externalities so that direct government intervention is necessary to maintain amenity supply and to reveal demand for them. They are:

- *Regulations:* The aim is to determine and/or reassign rights relating to the ownership and use of amenities, since these rights are often not clearly defined or need to be reassigned to promote the valorisation of amenities or to avoid further degradation. Although the clear definition or reassignment of property rights may facilitate the establishment of markets in the case of a private good amenity, regulations are often imposed to restrict the individual ownership over an amenity: society is considered to hold the property right. Thus the general function of regulations is to internalise public goods and/or externalities at the expense of providers.

- *Financial incentives:* The aim is to pay for the supply of amenities and to tax actions which have a negative impact on amenities in order to internalise such actions. When an amenity is a public good and/or an externality, governments are required to create substitute markets: to send demand signals to providers on behalf of potential beneficiaries.

The emergence of urban amenity policies

In general, policies to improve the competitiveness of cities are emphasising their comparative advantages in terms of knowledge infrastructure and the range and variety of interactions among diverse economic actors. As noted above, innovation-led policies of the type discussed earlier in this report are generally applicable in urban regions, and the main successful models related to these approaches tend to be found in and around metropolitan areas (though not exclusively so). Nonetheless, governments continue to emphasise the challenges that many cities face in restructuring former industrial economies and the problems of maintaining economic and social vitality in particular areas of cities (whether inner city or suburbs). In such cases, there is a need to address issues of the wider urban environment as well as addressing policies for the enterprise sector directly. In this regard, there is a close relation between the issues and responses of rural amenity policies and those being developed in cities. The transition path of Busan, Korea is a good example (see Box 1.14).

The urban amenity issue is exemplified by the common problem of how to regenerate historic city centres. The motivation for regenerating historical districts is, on the one hand, a social question. Residents must appreciate the value of their cultural heritage in order to give a mandate for public authorities to make the necessary investments to preserve and restore. This has not always been apparent, with the extent of the loss of patrimony only becoming a matter of wide public concern when it is almost too late to reverse the process. In many cases, private national and international foundations have been responsible for preserving specific buildings and lobbying for more active intervention from governments. Once there is a more general recognition of the need to safeguard the cultural heritage and once the pressures and threats to the areas concerned have been accepted, then governments have acted with a range of regulatory instruments and grants to redevelop individual buildings and, more recently, whole neighbourhoods. The expense of such programmes and the limited ability of public authorities to go beyond addressing physical decline and address functional obsolescence have tended to undermine the outcomes from these programmes. In many US and European cities, large scale investments have been made to remodel industrial, often river-front or canal-front sites in order to, on the one hand, preserve decaying industrial heritage sites, and, on the other, to rejuvenate depressed city centre areas. These have had very mixed success, with property re-development in some cases triggering little spillover for the wider central city area. The weakness of many of these earlier initiatives was the lack of emphasis on the subsequent viability of retail and entertainment businesses, the principal users of commercial space in such zones. As a result of these experiences, there has been a shift to a stronger emphasis on the economic motivation for regeneration. Here the issue of amenities and ways of developing markets or quasi-markets for public goods becomes significant.

The common denominator in most urban regeneration projects in Europe and the US is the recognition that physical renovation is not sufficient but that

Box 1.14. Reorientation of industrial cities: the port city of Busan, Korea

Given the possibility for Busan's port volumes to plateau or even decline, it would be prudent to avoid the potential risks of overinvestment strategy over the long term. Port cities increasingly follow a path of development that can be schematised in three main phases, from pre-industrial to industrial and on to knowledge-based economies. Most large port cities in Pacific Asia are in the second phase, which is reflected in the primary importance given to port infrastructure investment geared for larger ships and wider logistical networks that are shipping-intensive. In the future, however, there will be a clear push to make the port more relevant to needs not directly related to shipping. These needs include amenities and service industries. There is increasing international awareness of this nearly inevitable shift.* And the rise of competing ports in China may in the long term lead Busan and other similarly situated ports in advanced economies more decisively in this direction. Most port cities are endeavouring to create more integrated city-port linkages and have also shown renewed concern for the environment and urban liveability. Busan should take due note of these trends in shaping its own planning decisions.

* The 7th International Conference of Cities and Ports in 2000 concluded that "port cities must now create investment and development programs that will enhance their quality of life as a desirable maritime or riverside metropolis. Local environmental resources must be preserved and the social and cultural development of the local community supported if sustainability is to be achieved. Each port city must define a policy for overall development that takes on broad ecological and social issues". The International Association of Cities and Ports (IACP), which is dedicated to promoting "real partnerships between these two 'worlds' – the city and its port", has as its theme for the 2004 annual conference "Modernity and Identity". It stated that "the modernity of a port city is then expressed in its capacity to participate in these new worldwide networks, to integrate them in the logics of their political, economic and social choices, to translate them in terms of infrastructure, of equipment and installations and of professional training. Responding to this requirement of modernity is that of identity. Keeping its cultural reference points, valorising its acquired advantages and affirming its ambitions in terms of sustainable development and quality of life are the indispensable corollaries to any development project".

Table 1.4. Port city transition

Port City Region	→ Port City Transition →		
	1) Pre-industrial	2) Labour-intensive export industry	3) Amenity-rich, knowledge-intensive
Port Functions	Simple sea-land interface	Logistical distribution platforms (*e.g.* among industrial estates and export processing zone facilities)	Region wide intermodal nodes in international supply chain networks
City Region Economy	Commercial centre, primary product export	Branch plant light industry and assembly operations; local management functions of global firms.	Knowledge-based, diversified high technology "learning regions" with headquarter functions and amenities as attractions for investment.
Urban Design Focus	Port development and city development separated. Port as "dockland"; city as separate commercial centre. Emphasis on trunk road linkages to resource and agricultural hinterlands to ports.	Port development linked by trunk roads to new peri-urban industrial "growth poles" as globally-linked enclaves. City hosts local TNC management functions with focus on raising central city skylines and providing for massive suburbanization of residential population.	Port as "riverside" landscapes integrated into city design; city as amenity-rich, historically-rich landscapes with multiple locations for public engagement and life-long learning; shift from metropolis to post-metropolitan urban regional networks

Source: *OECD Territorial Review of Busan* (2005).

economic and social dynamics have to be "invented" for these areas. For example, the grouping of retail outlets in or around historical areas effectively provides a "backdrop" for bars and restaurants, cultural and entertainment facilities, etc. In many US cities, historical buildings have been renovated for use by creative arts – as dance studios, artists' studios, etc. In these cases, public authorities and private developers gamble on a strong link between different forms of culture (architecture, arts, etc.) and evolutions in patterns of consumption.

The idealised "chain" is: people increasingly value living in or visiting historic areas, the number of residents and visitors increases, the commercial value of these locations increases, this draws in investment to create commercial and residential spaces. In this scenario, civil society guides the public sector with respect to the desires and aspirations of citizens, the public authorities put in place a regulatory framework and provide incentives, and

> Box 1.15. **The balance sheet of urban amenity promotion in Glasgow**
>
> Heritage and culture as catalysts for urban regeneration and economic growth are increasingly favoured options for European cities. The regeneration and economic development trajectory for the city of Glasgow was built on several important events beginning in 1988 with the UK National Garden Festival, a river based regeneration initiative. The Festival was an important event for the city. At a cost of £20 million to the public purse the event drew in some four million visitors to the city and marked the beginning of a new approach to urban regeneration in Glasgow. Cultural events became an integral part of the regeneration process as was seen elsewhere in Europe throughout the decade. In 1990, Glasgow was a European City of Culture, an event which captured the imagination of politicians and regeneration agencies alike. Nine million admissions were recorded, over half a million from outside the city, adding £80 million to the local economy. New landmark buildings such as the Glasgow Royal Concert Hall, a £28.5 million investment by Glasgow City Council, had a considerable impact. In 1996, the Glasgow Festival of Visual Arts generated £25 million of visitor expenditure with a net economic benefit of £5.5 million for the city economy. In 1999 Glasgow was City of Architecture and Design, which generated £20 million and resulted in the creation of 500 jobs. Investment in culture has continued as the city has developed a science museum, a strong cultural industries base and significant urban design improvements throughout the city.
>
> Source: OECD, *Urban Renaissance Review of Glasgow*.

the private sector reacts to changes in the local market for investment. Two recent OECD studies of urban regeneration policies in Belfast and Glasgow showed how each city has identified its major river (the Lagan and the Clyde respectively) as an underused amenity. In both cases, the riverfronts were the traditional industrial heart of the city and now a new functional relevance was needed in the two areas in order to attract back both investment and residents. The approach of the Laganside Corporation, which was responsible for implementing a development strategy was grounded in the premise that the scale of the area's needs required substantial private sector investment, but that the initial investment in infrastructure, land remediation and environmental improvements would have to come from the public sector. Once the commitment of the public authorities had been demonstrated, private sector investment and confidence was forthcoming.

Actions related to attractiveness of the region as an investment or residential location are of particular interest to policymakers insofar as they provide a coherent and convenient framework for regional investment strategies, particularly to the extent that they target upgrading endogenous assets and underdeveloped potential in a region. In this respect, greater use of the framework developed by OECD for rural amenities is relevant with respect to creation of markets for collective public goods and the tools for supporting collective action and public-private partnerships to transform urban land use patterns and regenerate decaying neighbourhoods. While analysis at the international level has tended to focus on amenities as a rural policy issue, there is growing interest in the "amenities as local public goods" concept applied to urban areas. Most of the same conceptual issues concerning the relation between amenities and development are equally applicable (synergy, antagonism and interdependence), as are many of the policy options (market creation, support for collective action regulatory and financial incentives for provision, etc.). More generally, they raise a number of important governance issues about how investment is made in urban areas and by whom.

Notes

1. Despite their general use in policy discourse, these assumptions are not all shared by opinion makers. Paul Krugman is perhaps the most prominent critic of the assertion that places are "like big corporations competing in the global marketplace", arguing that an over-emphasis on international competition ignores major differences between the characteristics and behaviour of a company and those of a country, notably that a country cannot go out of business and does not necessarily have to make an operating profit, and could provoke "un-economic" policy responses (notably protectionist policies and rejection of free trade principles). A related problem with the implication that places compete is the assumption that firms and the regions or countries in which they are located share similar objectives – wealth creation, employment creation, in some

definitions sustainable development, and so on. This may be true in some cases, but is certainly not true in all. In a global economy, firms are not tied to specific places and their profit motivation is not the same as the wealth and employment creation motivation of a region in particular.Even if the interests of firms and those of local and national authorities are not always synonymous, they are nonetheless closely related.

2. Michael Porter asserts that "firms gain competitive advantage where their home base allows and supports the rapid accumulation of specialised assets and skills… Nations succeed in particular industries because their home environment is the most dynamic…".

3. These interdependencies are similar to the concept of "social capital". Social capital is a set of intangible factors such as trust, mores and networks which contribute to the overall capital stock.

4. The two areas where this channel seems to be particularly strong is technology transfer and human capital formation. Through their linkages with domestic enterprises – on recent evidence, mainly their direct suppliers – foreign-owned enterprises share know-how with the local business community. As for human capital, foreign-owned enterprises tend to "spin off" trained employees, and in many cases also managers, whose specialist skills then benefit unrelated enterprises or serve as a source of entrepreneurship in the local economy.

5. Some research has suggested that US technology parks have more than double the number of support staff as similar facilities in either Europe or Japan, with the conclusion being that the US cases place more emphasis on active support for new businesses.

6. The current Industrial Cluster initiative in Japan and the initiative in Scotland cover relatively large urban regions and emphasise an array of well-funded services. Other more regional initiatives, such as that in the Arve valley in France and the city of Tempere in Finland, covered more restricted areas and provided more limited ranges of services (Raines, 2003).

7. *www.dti.gov.uk/iese/international_comparisons.pdf*.

8. One example is Busan University, which has created a think tank called the Asian Institute for Regional Innovation (AIRI). This think tank not only organises research projects and seminars but also participates in the activities of regional innovation councils in the Busan area, implements various education programmes for regional innovation and networks with overseas universities and research institutes (Japan, China, United States).

9. Valuation approaches have also come to the fore in efforts to quantify the environmental damage caused by oil spills for the purpose of determining costs to be borne by the polluter. Economic valuation is widely used in OECD countries as a way of assessing values (usually monetary) to goods that have no markets. Valuation methods are used to support or argue against projects and policy choices. The political relevance of the debate stems from the technical and ethical difficulties of assessing the value of non-market goods. This means that the validity of much of the information presented to or by governments, in defense of key arguments in domestic and international policy debates, is often contested. Economists have developed a variety of techniques to value non-market environmental and cultural amenities consistent with the valuation of marketed goods; *i.e.* based on individual preferences.

10. Even when the methodology may be sound, the fact that many estimates (particularly of non-use values) are based on hypothetical "contingent valuation" surveys, means that the results cannot be taken too literally. There may be large differences between what people say they are willing to pay and what people actually disburse. To test this disparity, a willingness-to-pay mail survey that was followed by an invoice requesting the sum that the respondent had claimed to be willing to pay. While many people paid, the discrepancy was nonetheless large.

Part II

Governance

Introduction

Regional competitiveness rests on networked forms of production. The corollary of this assessment is that firms are more dependent, especially when it concerns SMEs, on the local environment in which they are located. In order to develop and prosper, firms need to use all sorts of goods and services that are provided in different ways. When these are made available within a particular geographical context they can be considered as "local collective competition goods" (Crouch et al., 2001). They may concern availability of relevant skills, access to information related to technical evolution or external markets, the sharing of a territorial label, etc. These collective goods and services provide competitive capacity to the actors located in the place. Their combination constitutes specific answers to the competitiveness challenges faced by local areas: workforce, lifestyle, financial and above all informational capacities.[1] These collective goods do not appear at random. Their provision must be ensured by social or political arrangements, strongly linked to the central government regional policy (objectives and means), that is, by forms of multi-level governance.

Governance across levels of government – or "multilevel governance" – has become a major issue in territorial policy making and was recognised as one of the central elements of territorial policy making at the OECD High Level Meeting on Innovation and Effectiveness in Territorial Development Policy in 2003.[2] Multilevel governance, understood here as the exertion of authority across levels of government, has changed over the last two decades. Decentralisation has made local and regional governments more powerful and increased their capacity to operate their own development and management policies. The emergence of private actors that take part in policy making and the increased number of public-private partnerships has made the stakeholders' pattern more colourful but also more complicated. Local and regional governments – much more exposed to global competition than twenty years ago – want to have a bigger say in the setting and implementation of national policy measures. People at the local and regional level put pressure on the outcome of policy delivery and require that publicly funded programmes have a real and positive impact on their lives. And finally, the main objective of regional policy is moving away from redistribution and towards growth enhancement. Taking such secular trends into account, management and governance of public development and related programmes have become more complex and more demanding, requiring a rethinking of how national and sub-national governments should collaborate.

New forms of governance targeting local and regional competitiveness are oriented towards co-operation. It can be vertical, mirroring the linkages between lower and higher levels of government (Chapter 4) or horizontal, for example between communes or between regions (Chapter 5). Co-operative linkages also concern various types of stakeholders at a given level of governance – essentially public sector and private sector actors (profit or non-profit) (Chapter 6). In practice, these different forms of co-ordination can be integrated in one and the same system, as is the case for example with "micro-regions" in Mexico or the Czech Republic. Chapter 7 will underline three issues common to these governance matters.

4. Coordination between the different levels of government: transfers, contracting practices and incentives

The first part of this report demonstrates that strategies to promote competitiveness are multi-sectoral and involve many different actors. The central government intervenes in these mechanisms by supporting public service delivery according to standards set at the national level. Local public services are, as we have seen, an essential feature of the attractiveness of the territories. To let the supply of these services depend on decisions made by local authorities and their financial resources would present important risks of coherence. Indeed, local and regional authorities could choose to compete among themselves, in order to attract private investment, by reducing local taxes (or constraints on environmental norms), which would in turn force them to reduce local public services ("race to the bottom" issues).

However, the central government's role consists of more than simply distributing grants and setting standards. All the more so when local collective competition goods are created, which depend to a large extent on local input such as setting up a network of actors or local contacts. Under these conditions, policies directed at regions and local areas should be undertaken in coordination with regional and local governments. The central government should thus also intervene to facilitate co-operation among different actors, using, for example, fiscal instruments to encourage co-operation among municipalities, encouraging diversity in the partnerships that support local projects, involving the private sector, etc. Introducing competition among local projects to obtain grants from central government can also be an effective way of encouraging partnerships at local level.

Nevertheless, the dependence upon central resources and expertise is partial. In a context of regional specificities and research for knowledge-based assets, local and regional authorities are often best placed to identify the possible unexploited factors of growth and the measures to take in order to implement their promotion. Bottom-up initiatives are required rather than top down decisions to be implemented locally. What organisational devices can enable both the participation of central and regional levels of government and co-operative rather than hierarchical relations? In this report we examine the contractual types of relations among levels of government.

Decentralisation and transfers

Although in theory local authorities should make use of their own revenue to provide local public services, all countries – including the most decentralised ones – have public finance relations between levels of government that take the form of intergovernmental transfers. Through these transfers, central governments try to ensure that all local authorities can fulfil their responsibility for a certain number of public services whose standards are usually set at national level. The central government supplements the local budgets by:

- grants earmarked to specific types of local public services,
- among these earmarked grants, some are proportional grants depending on the amount that local authorities are committed to spend[3] (via a matching rate that is supposed to compensate local authorities for the extent of benefit spillovers across jurisdictional boundaries),
- general purpose grants not earmarked for a specific purpose (by assessing the amount of these grants according to different formulas tied to the demographic or geographic features of the area).[4]

The different types of transfers have an impact on how public decision-makers behave at local and regional level. If the transfers in question are earmarked grants and if they are proportional (according to the terminology used by the Council of Europe, 2004) the local authorities will have limited room to manoeuvre in their spending. On the other hand, if the transfers are non-proportional or general purpose grants, there is much more freedom left for local decision-making.

Trends in intergovernmental transfers highlight a complex reshaping of relations across level of governments.

First, there is an observable trend to increase the relative weight of central government transfers in local and regional financing in the great majority of countries (see Figures 2.1 and 2.2).

The two graphs can be summarised as follows:

1. The degree of decentralisation varies greatly across OECD countries. For instance, the sub-national share of total government expenditures varies from less than 6% up to more than 50%. The constitutional framework for

Figure 2.1. **Indicators of fiscal decentralisation in OECD countries: sub-national government share in general government revenues and expenditures, percentages, 2002**[1]

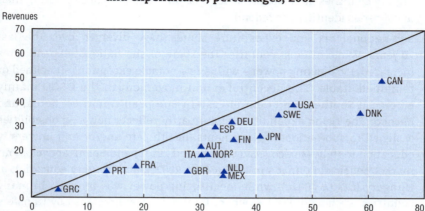

Note: Revenues include direct and indirect taxes as well as non-tax revenues received by regional and local governments and are expressed as a share of revenues received by the general government. Expenditure corresponds to total expenditure by regional and local governments expressed as a share of general government expenditure.
1. Or latest year available: 2000 for Japan, 2001 for France and Portugal.
2. Mainland only. Data exclude revenues from oil production.
Source: OECD, National Accounts database, Statistics Norway, Statistics Canada, US Bureau of Economic Analysis.

Figure 2.2. **Changes in the share of sub-national governments in total public revenues and spending**
Changes expressed in percentage points, 1985[1]-2002[2]

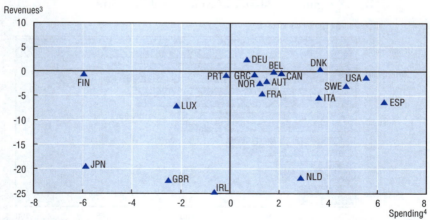

1. Or earliest year available: 1986 for Ireland, 1987 for the United Kingdom, 1990 for Japan, Luxembourg and Netherlands, 1991 for Germany, 1993 for Sweden, 1995 for Greece, Portugal and Spain.
2. Or latest year available: 1997 for Canada and the United States, 1996 for Ireland and 1998 for Portugal.
3. Excluding transfers received from other levels of government.
4. Excluding transfers paid to other levels of government.
Source: OECD National Accounts data. Statistics Norway.

government in a country – federal or unitary – has surprisingly little impact on the extent of decentralisation. Sub-national governments in some unitary countries are responsible for a larger share of public spending than in countries identified as federal.

2. Sub-national tax and expenditure shares have diverged over the last 20 years. While in most countries the share of sub-national expenditures increased, local taxing power – with a few notable exceptions – declined or remained stable. The decentralisation movement in the OECD mainly embraced Southern and Central-Eastern European countries, Korea, and Mexico. The rising expenditure share partly reflects new responsibilities assigned to sub-national governments (health care and/or non-university education in Italy, Mexico (OECD, 2003a and 2001a) and Spain, active labour market policies in Canada in 1996 (OECD, 2002c), and primary education in Hungary (OECD, 2001c), while local taxing power was reduced in many countries, such as in France, where local taxes were replaced by transfers (OECD, 2002d).

3. Most countries exhibit sub-national expenditures that are larger than sub-national tax receipts and this gap is widening over time. This points to the existence of large inter governmental transfer schemes. The size and structure of intergovernmental grants and their management are becoming crucial issues of multilevel governance.

Second, non-earmarked transfers are well diffused (with the notable exception of the United States) (see Figure 2.3).

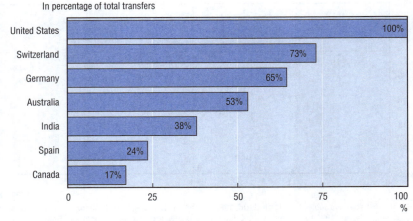

Figure 2.3. **Shares of conditional transfers**

Source: Department of Finance, Canada, 1998.

Third, applied research has shown in many cases that matching rates broadly exceeded any possible spillover measures (Oates, 1999; Inman, 1988).

According to the prevailing economic thought on local finance these trends could have diverging results. Reducing the financial independence of local authorities has the advantage of allowing the central government to have more control over the growth and distribution of resources. However, it operates as a kind of disincentive to local government from taking responsibility vis-à-vis their electors and from providing local public services that are cost-effective. However, the fact that most of the transfers are non-specific carries the opposite risk, reducing the powers of control available to central government. What is more, this type of financing places a heavy burden of responsibility on local players who do not necessarily have the capacity to handle it. At the same time, these trends have advantages, too, especially in terms of reducing the transaction costs associated with transfers (administrative costs in particular).

While these trends in intergovernmental transfers could be quickly regarded as out of control, they deserve a more in depth and careful analysis. Of course, fiscal decisions that are often outcomes of negotiations between central and "local" authorities could be seen as the result of politically driven criteria that could be different from the result of weighing benefits and costs of prospective public programs. However, viewing public decision-making as something that should result automatically from the application of normative guiding principles, rather than being the subject of negotiation, could be equally considered out of touch with reality. In many cases, the central government contribution is no longer just used for revenue balancing but rather for competences that are shared across levels of government and cannot be assigned once for all as well as for inciting regions to valorise their comparative advantages and enhance their competitiveness. In this context, policy strategies are impacted by uncertainty about decisions. With asymmetry of information between the "principal" (the central government) and the "agents" (the sub-national ones),[5] and with the necessity of dialogue between different actors, appropriate strategies for development are more likely to emerge from having plurality of participation in decision-making (with different types of actors, central, regional and local) as well as in policy implementation.

The regional development contracts

Fiscal relations across levels of government can include, among other things, institutional mechanisms to support transfers of funds between the upstream and downstream levels of government. In particular, there is growing interest in contracts between levels of government as a practice that could provide a response to central government involvement in local spending and bring different partners together with a common focus. Contracts set out the goals, the nature of the transfers, the conditions attached to the transfers and the obligations of the different parties. While they can provide support for some redistribution initiatives (between regions and municipalities) on the part of central government, they are not designed as *ex post facto* compensatory tools for adjustment, but rather they have to do with the central government playing an upfront role in regional and local development strategies. At the same time, contracts can valorise the role of local decision-makers, their proximity to problems and resources of a region and therefore their capacity to better target the initiatives and utilise untapped development potential. This involves opening up contractual negotiations to local third parties, beyond just actors in the public sector: business representatives, private citizens, interest groups, etc. Contracts can help to harness diversity and develop the particular features of each region within the framework of the desired consistency at national level. The fact that they are negotiated means they have more in common with planning initiatives shared between the different levels of government than with a kind of "homogenisation" of regional and local situations.

Contractual arrangements can be found in all kinds of countries with a democratic regime, they cannot be ascribed to a specific type of State organisation,[6] and include all or part of complex mechanisms such as:

- *Vertical relations* with several varying dimensions including financial transfers (that for European countries also includes the supra-national level of the Union).
- *Local horizontal relations.* Several contracts involve the participation of different local authorities as well as the private sector.[7]
- *Central horizontal relations,* i.e. co-ordination between the different ministries involved in regional policy in order to overcome the traditional isolation of sectoral policies.[8]
- *Conditions and incentives arrangement.* In order to comply with the conditions of contracts, regions have to propose projects which are very detailed in terms of lead time, technology content, environmental impact, costs, etc. Moreover, in various countries, contracts are financially underpinned by transfers dependent on the success of regional policy and development programmes. The conditions that go with these transfers vary[9] but, as with all types of contract, they shape the incentives influencing the behaviour of local government.

The 3 types of contracts in existence with regard to regional development

There are three types of contract in the field of regional development. Planning and programme contracts integrate a number of policies and programmes in the territory covered. Implementation contracts mainly concern contractual arrangements devoted to the devolution of regional or local planning to sub-national levels of governments. Co-operation contracts organise co-operation between different parties to carry out a specific programme or project, establishing their reciprocal commitments. In the latter case, contracts do not reflect a principal/agent type of relationship since each partner has in principle an equal position in the co-operation.

Planning and programme contracts

There are several programme contracts (especially in Switzerland with the programme contracts in regional public transport and the programme contracts in forest management (TR Switzerland, 2002). We will mainly be looking at one of the most representative mechanisms in the field, especially because of the increasingly multisectoral nature of the commitments: the French CPERs (TR France, forthcoming).

The State-region plan contract (*contrat de plan Etat-région*, CPER) became a key instrument of the regional development policy just a few years after its creation. Contracts have been passed with all regions for the periods 1984-88, 1989-93, 1994-98 (postponed until the end of 1999) and 2000-06. The contract is a detailed document, setting out a series of policies and programmes which will be carried out for a certain period. The central government and the region jointly finance the projects in the contract, and, recent contracts have included contributions of infra-regional governments and European structural funds. The contract includes a financial appendix stating the precise amount of the financial commitment of each party for the period covered by the contract. Contracts do not necessarily imply budgetary transfers between the central government and local governments; instead they usually stress the responsibilities and commitments of each party, while providing a detailed description of the purpose of each measure.

The decentralisation laws have had a significant impact on the State-region plan contracts. As regions have acquired more power over the decision-making process, the contracts have expanded to include new fields, often with larger budgets (increasingly financed by regional and local authorities) and new actors such as representatives of civil society. As a result of this process, planning at the national level has been entirely replaced by State-region plan contracts, which provide the only framework for forward-looking and consultative policy-making.

Although the first contracts were mainly devoted to infrastructure projects and the modernisation of industries, the second generation of contracts dealt with a broader range of issues, including regional innovation and urban planning. During the 90s, the budget for these contracts increased dramatically by over 45%, partly as a result of contributions from new sources such as local authorities and the European funds. In addition, the central government sought to enable poorer regions to compete on a more equal footing by providing them with a larger share of resources through the contracts (which was seen as a supplementary instrument for equalisation), depending on their rate of unemployment, employment perspectives and fiscal capacity indicators. The idea was to promote local development through the contract as a complement to other more traditional programmes using compensation subsidies. The current contract (2000-2006) reinforces this trend. Today the budget is more important and the regional contribution slightly exceeds that of the central government. Public investment under the contracts accounts for 15 to 20% of the central government budget and for 5 to 30% of the regional council budgets. For instance, in the Ile de France (Paris and its neighbouring region) the regional council contributes more than 60% and the central government 39%. Central government participation ranges from 39% (Ile de France) to more than 63% (Limousin), reflecting the government's attempts to enable less competitive regions to catch up. The ministries that contribute the most to regional programmes through the contracts are the ministry of infrastructure, transportation and housing (40%), followed by the ministry of education (17%) and the ministry of agriculture (9%). However, the great majority of the different ministries are now involved in State-region planning contracts.

The current planning contract is structured around four areas: sustainable development (which has led policy-makers to favour investments in collective transportation and railways rather than roads), employment in all sectors, solidarity (which has led to urban renewal programmes, improvements in the delivery of public services, etc.) and "immaterial functions" (such as education, research and development, ICT diffusion, etc.). The current contract contains a new system for classifying projects into the following categories: "regional issues" (*volet régional*), "territorial matters" (*volet territorial* for infra regional issues), and "inter-regional matters". At least 25% of the contract's budget must be devoted to territorial matters.

Organisational setting: The implementation of the planning contract necessitates the participation of various actors; central, regional and local authorities, their representatives and some bodies for intermediation:

Figure 2.4. **Organisational structure for regional contracts**

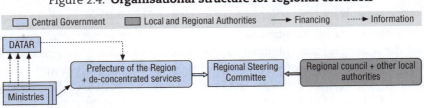

The planning contract is the result of a long process of mutual commitment between two different groups of actors: 1) the elected local and regional authorities, and the "development actors" in the region (firms, associations, etc.) under the co-ordination of the regional authority and 2) the regional "prefect" who is not elected but designated by the State and an "actor of intermediation". All the regional planned projects are co-ordinated by the Delegation for Territorial Management and Regional Action (DATAR, *délégation à l'aménagement du territoire et à l'action régionale*). Different ministries form steering committees to coordinate the actions taken by the central and regional governments in different sectors at the regional level. It is important to note that, under the current generation of contracts, when dealing with territorial development, inter-municipal structures direct transversal projects instead of the steering committees.

Challenges: Indeed, a number of important problems exist. Delays in the implementation of decisions contained in the contracts may necessitate their extension beyond 2006. However underperformance can rarely be put down to a breach of contract in the sense of a desire to escape from one's obligations. It is more likely the consequence of delays in availability of funds, as a consequence of budgetary regulation, or of changes in circumstances that mean funds are reallocated, or of programmes the costs of which have been underestimated or preliminary studies not completed. Aside from such incidents, which may admittedly be serious, contracts are performed. When there is failure to perform, there is hardly a single case where one of the parties has made a claim in the administrative court; the claimant has always been a third party. Indeed, neither central government nor the region has any interest in leaving the solution of a conflict to the courts, not least because of the length of the procedure. Basically, they are forced to cooperate because of their legal competences. As a result, there is nothing to be gained from obtaining the satisfaction of a judgment on one matter, at the expense of ongoing relations. On the contrary, the preferred course is to seek compensation by negotiation on another subject. In addition, various regional authorities have complained that the central government is not honouring its financial commitments. On the other hand, some critics see such arrangements as being more an instrument of State devolution than as imparting any real impetus in partnership terms. A negative aspect is that it remains too much top-down due to a stronger negotiating power of the State with the consequences that priority actions do not differ significantly from one region to another.

French authorities are aware of these problems. An evaluation of the CPER device, currently in process, has generated a number of debatable recommendations. Among them, the proposition to re-centre the planning contracts around a limited number of structural policies is a crucial one but a lot of observers believe that reforming the device in this way will threaten local initiative. Another important recommendation is related to the insufficiency of the evaluating process which could perhaps be improved thanks to a more transparent and independent council for evaluation. Other financial considerations have also led them to recommend greater "fungibility" of the budgets. A last important recommendation is that in order to strategically reinforce the long term coherence of the various CPER a "national scheme with a long term perspective" could be set up. The region will be in charge of a "strategic document of orientation" which would consolidate its role as leading intermediary structure (between national and local levels).

Implementation contracts

These contracts are provided by numerous laws in France, VINEX covenants in the Netherlands, contractual arrangements for the implementation of regional planning in Germany, or the programme contract in Italy which is a contract made by the competent central administration, large firms, associations of small and medium enterprises, representatives of industrial districts, for the implementation of activities under a negotiated programme. In what follows we will focus on the Netherlands and Germany.

The Netherlands. The Netherlands define themselves as a "decentralised unitary state", with three government levels: the central government, provinces and municipalities. It is also characterised by "co-government" practices (medebewind); this means that policy-making generally involves central government and local government in most policy fields, partly because of the relatively small size of the country. Decision-making processes usually include consensus building, even when it takes a lot of time. There is no fragmentation as in France. Due to its high density of population, the Netherlands has developed country wide spatial planning. Contracts have appeared as an instrument for the implementation of the national plan, and may be considered as a form of "co-government".

The national plan is adopted by a key planning decision of the central government; concrete policy planning decisions for parts of the plan have to be complied with by local plans. However, for the Supplement to the Fourth Report on Country Planning (*Vierde Nota over de Ruimtelijke Ordening Extra – VINEX*), adopted in 1991 and still in force, the government decided to pass contracts with provinces and municipalities, including the regional bodies (sub-provincial in the Netherlands). To simplify the negotiation, the central government passed contracts directly with the four main cities, whereas it passed a contract with the association of provinces to delegate to provinces the contracts with 18 other urban areas. These contracts included housing, urban extensions, green areas, public transports. As a counterpart for financial support by the central government, local governments had to use their prerogatives, in particular as regards planning, in accordance with the guidance of the national plan.

The multilateral contracts ROM (*Ruimtelijke Ordening en Milieu* – Planning and Environment) are another example devoted to fragile areas. There is a consultation round on the basis of a planning project. A contract results from the agreement expressed by all parties. The procedure is open to private bodies, by contrast with VINEX covenants. Their content includes a large variety of subjects, because the strategy was based on the achievement of a package deal: each party had to reach a satisfactory agreement on a subject in order to commit to the whole.

At present, and since 1999, the Fifth Report is being prepared and should be decided soon. As before, there is no say on covenants on the planning documents. Covenants are not planning instruments but implementation instruments. It is too soon to anticipate whether and how again the implementation of the Fifth Report would proceed through covenants.

Germany. In *Germany* contractual arrangements still have little place in the planning system, or a very specific one. Regarding the relationships between the Federation and the *Länder*, the institutional scene absorbs most of the political agreements. The *Bundesrat* secures the co-decision right of *Länder* governments in federal policies, and those which have an impact on economic development and planning policies of the *Länder* (common tasks of the article 91a of the Basic Law) are managed by joint committees in which the *Länder* governments have collective control over decisions. Otherwise, there are 13 inter-ministerial committees linking the Federation and the *Länder* over almost all policy fields; they have been set up by treaties which lay down their working rules. However, deliberations of these committees may result in collective agreements for the implementation of specific policies by all *Länder*. An example is the "administrative agreement" on the financial support of the Federation to urban planning measures of 19 December 2001 and 9 April 2002; this support has to be transferred to municipalities on the basis of their projects by the *Land* government.[10] The procedural and deliberative mode of exchange between government levels is usually described in Germany as the expression of the *Gegenstromprinzip*, that is to say the principle of "reciprocal flows". In the institutional structure of Germany a significant development of contractual arrangements for planning is probably not needed.

Co-operation contracts

Their purpose is to govern co-operation between different parties carrying out a specific programme or project, laying down their reciprocal commitments; most contractual arrangements under the laws in Italy and

Spain belong to this category. In Spain as in Italy, in contrast to Germany, contractual arrangements have increased tremendously in the last decade, probably as a result of the devolution of responsibilities to regions. In many respects, the situation in Italy is similar to the situation of Spain, but the differences need to be pointed out. The development of contractual arrangements below the regional level is important, whereas contractual relations between central government and regions are less developed. Italian regions seem to be less involved in national policy-making than their Spanish counterparts. Furthermore, the Italian legal tradition is reluctant towards public law contracts, in contrast to Spain where the administrative law covers a wide sphere of legal relations, including contracts.

Spain. In the absence of an institutionalised participation of regions in the national policy-making process in Spain, there is a proliferation of councils in which regions are involved in key decisions affecting their interests (for example: on fiscal and financial policy, on health, on research and technology...), of sectoral conferences, and other mixed bodies. As a whole there are more than 400 mixed bodies in which policies, projects and financing are discussed between regions and central government. These relationships have also developed through various sorts of contracts. The law has attempted to organise and clarify this process (national laws 12/1983 and 30/1992). The latter piece of legislation establishes three kinds of contractual arrangements between the central government and regions:

- agreements passed within sectoral conferences, which are deemed to involve all regions;
- co-operation agreements (*convenios de colaboración*): they are bilateral, can be passed between public administrations, they have to provide for funding and can establish a permanent corporate structure;
- joint plans and programmes (*planes y programas conjuntos*): they are contracts between the administration of a region and the general administration at the central level in order to achieve common objectives in the field of shared competences; they are also bilateral and may be combined with a co-operation agreement.

Italy. The contract system began with the transfer of central government competences to ordinary regions in 1970. The presidential decree No. 616 of 24 July 1977 provides for contractual arrangements following this transfer: between regions for activities overlapping their borders; between central government, regions and other local governments for the use of school infrastructure, and between central government and regions for public works deviating from local planning rules. The Constitutional Court confirmed this possibility as a response to the need for close co-operation between central government and regions. Later on, other laws provided for contracts between central government, regions and local governments for their implementation, in particular the law No. 64 of 1986 for development programmes of the Mezzogiorno.

But, with the laws No. 142 and 241/1990, contracts or agreements became a general means of administrative action. The first law gave legal effect to municipal autonomy, and the second one is the first general law on administrative procedure. The development of contractual arrangements led to a new system of classification with the law No. 662 of 23 December 1996 (Art. 2, par. 203), which is still in force:

- the negotiated programme, between public subjects, or public and private subjects, but for a common purpose;
- the institutional programme agreement: includes a financial programme and a multi-annual operational programme;
- the framework programme agreement: is used for a complex programme, determines the commitments of each party, provides for the necessary service conferences and the implementation agreements;
- the territorial covenant (*patto territoriale*): it is an intervention programme agreed by local governments, social partners and other public or private parties for a development programme similar to those covered by framework programme agreements;
- the area programme: this is an operational instrument agreed between public administrations (national, regional, local…), representatives of workers and employers aimed at interventions to support job creation in the area.

Additionally, the programme agreement (*accordo di programma*) of the law No. 142 is still in force in article 34 of the new code of local government (*Texto unico delle leggi sull'ordinamento degli enti locali*, D.Lgs No. 267, 18 August 2000). Its purpose is to carry out public works, or programmes requiring the integration of the activities of different public administrations; the initiative belongs to the executive of the region, of the province or of the municipality, and gives rise to a service conference which verifies that the agreement can be achieved. The agreement needs the formal approval of the president of the region or, as the case may be, of the province or of the municipality. In case of conflict, the regional administrative court is competent. Programme agreements have become the most common contractual arrangement practised in Italy.

Canada. A similar approach has been adopted by Canada with the Labour Market Development Agreements and the Infrastructure Canada Programme which are Federal-Provincial-Partnerships.

Federal Provincial Partnerships in active employment policy. After a request from provinces to give them more control over labour market programming, the federal government in 1996 offered to turn over responsibility for active labour market programmes to the provinces. The offer encompassed the transfer of CAD 1.5 billion in 1997-1998 and 3 620 full time equivalent staff from federal to provincial administrations. In the two years that followed, agreements were negotiated between the federal government and most of the provinces. As of June 2001, Labour Market Development Agreements (LMDAs) have been negotiated with all the provinces and territories except Ontario. The Agreements are of two types: the first provides for a "full transfer" of authority to the province/territory, the second type is designated Co-management where there is no transfer of staff or funds. Under the "transfer" LMDAs, provinces and territories assume responsibility for delivery of active labour market assistance programmes similar to those described as Employment Benefits and Support Measures (EBSM) in the Employment Insurance Act. The Co-management LMDAs involve an innovative partnership between federal and provincial agencies administering the EBSMs. Preliminary findings from eleven completed formative evaluations indicate that LMDAs contribute to partnerships and the harmonisation of programmes and services and to local flexibility. Factors that have contributed to partnerships include a strong willingness to work together and maintain client service during implementation. In some situations, co-operation has uncovered opportunities for efficiencies and economies. Evaluations in most jurisdictions indicated duplication had decreased or remained the same as prior to the LMDA. Moreover, over 75% of EBSMs participants rated service as good or excellent. These results confirm that LMDAs are being used to assist eligible clients for employment benefits. Issues for further investigation include: the need to assess longer-term results, how to further improve co-ordination, and potential gaps in programming for non-Employment Insurance eligible clients.

We could also mention a more recent programme concerning infrastructure: *The Infrastructure Canada Programme* which is designed so that dedicated funding is provided over several fiscal years. The Infrastructure Canada Programme was the successor to the Canada Infrastructure Works Programme (CIWP), which ran from 1994-1999. Infrastructure Canada's principle focus is on "green" municipal infrastructure, such as municipal water, wastewater, solid waste management including, recycling, and improving energy efficiency in buildings. Secondary priorities include local transportation, cultural and recreational facilities, infrastructure that supports tourism, affordable housing, rural and remote telecommunications, and the provision of high-speed Internet access for public institutions. The programme is governed through federal-provincial/territorial agreements that provide for administration by management committees composed of two provincial and federal representatives. Each committee is headed by a federal co-chair and a provincial co-chair. The management committees in two provinces also include municipal representatives. In several other provinces municipal representatives are consulted in project assessment and selection. The federal share of funding under the programme (approximately one-third of eligible costs) was allocated to provinces and territories on the basis of the share of Canada's population and the share of Canada's unemployment. Each of these components is equally weighted. The remaining share of funds can come from provincial and local governments as well as non-governmental sources including, for example, public private partnerships. Generally, provincial governments contribute another third of costs, and local governments the remainder. Funding priorities were determined through negotiated agreements between the federal and provincial/territorial governments.

Advantages and disadvantages of contractual arrangements

Advantages

From the standpoint of multi-level governance, contractual arrangements have the following advantages:

- *Link regional and local policies to national priorities.* As such, contractual arrangements are measures accompanying further decentralisation while maintaining consistency in public policy making and implementation;[11]
- *Contribute to building local capacity.* In contractual arrangements, the "sub" level of government is not being looked upon as the mere recipient of a mandate granted to it. On the contrary, it is made responsible by virtue of its participation in decision-making and in the learning process. Therefore, these arrangements require a high level of participation, knowledge and competence on the part of local representatives. The *negotium* is at least as important as the *instrumentum* which results from it. This is particularly true for the cooperative type of contract and partly for the planning ones.
- Although less explicitly, *perform a legitimatisation function.* Whereas government by command is no longer practiced, contractual arrangements offer an opportunity for governments to submit their policies to the agreement of other authorities, which will have to comply with them, and to re-legitimise their authority through negotiation. This legitimisation effect is both relevant for the central and the regional level.
- *Help handling institutional fragmentation.* Contractual arrangements are meant to constitute a useful tool for improving co-ordination between different ministries acting at local level. As such, they are more developed

in more fragmented systems (France, Italy, Spain), where they tend to turn into an all-purpose instrument, than in more integrated systems (Germany, the Netherlands), where they tend to focus on specific purposes and have a more limited scope.[12] As for co-ordination between local jurisdictions, contractual arrangements can be an incentive for horizontal co-operation between local authorities.

- *Stabilisation of relationships.* Since the contract sets out long-term commitments, it allows each party to anticipate the decisions of its counterparts with more certainty. Even if this is not a guarantee, it reduces opportunistic behaviour and political risk to a minimum. Since most contractual arrangements involve financial commitments over several years they help overcome the drawbacks of the annual budgetary principle. The positive effect of the ability to anticipate is particularly manifest in implementation contracts. The reduction of opportunistic behaviour is a direct result of the co-operation. Both of these effects could be obtained in the planning and programme contracts if there were no uncertainty about the provision of resources by the central government (which is not completely the case in the French CPER).

- Contracts allow the burden of big projects and complex programmes to be shared, making possible the kind of operation which could not have been undertaken by an isolated government level.

- The contract is one of the procedures possible to get partners involved. Sharing the burden is also sharing the risks. This means, not only the financial ones, but also the political risks in case of difficulties: political criticism will not be possible from all those involved jointly. Therefore, contractual arrangements work as a kind of reassurance. However this impact is limited to the implementation contracts because decision making still belongs to the central levels.

Drawbacks and implementation problems

Contracts nevertheless have many drawbacks:

- They involve a high cost in terms of negotiation and execution (transaction costs, especially in the programming and co-operation types of contracts) and they risk being based on imperfect information.[13]

- User countries say that they tend to proliferate (France, Italy).

- The ministries in charge in the different countries seem reluctant to give up their prerogatives.

- While these negotiated mechanisms are supposed to allow a greater degree of flexibility than a hierarchical distribution of obligations, they may prove unresponsive to change where the parties are rigidly committed to fixed long-term programmes (that is especially true for planning and programme contracts).

- Another problem concerns the question of whether grants from the higher level of government should supply capital formation and/or current expenditure. The support of capital formation without the support of current expenditures linked to capital formation neglects the dynamic relationship between capital and current expenditures. Receiving regions may not be in a position to pay the current expenditure after they have invested in fixed capital, or they may neglect maintenance in order to obtain more capital grants in the future. Moreover, many development programmes aim at "soft" infrastructure but are technically or financially not considered capital formation, and thus receive no grants. In such a case, a bias towards capital grants neglects the formation of soft capital like capacity building or construction of regional knowledge systems.
- Furthermore, evaluation procedures are rarely provided for in advance, which means that it is not possible to measure the actual performance of this instrument which, moreover, often suffers from a lack of transparency. This limit especially concerns the co-operation contract (and partially the programming ones) since the evaluation of the co-operation per se is a complex task.
- It can also be said that the way infra-regional levels are positioned in contractual mechanisms directed by the upstream level often bears the signs of a power relationship. This underscores the risk of lack of downstream representation when appointing a regional intermediary leader.
- Without a regional leader, however, it would be more difficult to bind the local institutions in a contractual relationship with the central level, with the risk that the whole set-up of vertical relationships, if they were possible, would lack coherence. The leader should therefore be considered (and consider itself) more as an intermediary than the first in line.

Issues of policy making

Our discussion of contractual arrangements has produced a number of issues. While no perfect solution has emerged, one must note that countries which use such contractual arrangements are debating the need for an intermediary "leader" structure, the appropriate time period that contracts should cover and, finally, the appropriate geographic areas which they should cover.

The need for an intermediary "leader" structure

Appointing a local institution to act as "pilot" spokesman in contractual relations has both pros and cons. Should sub-regional levels be incorporated in an overall contractual framework in order to improve the consistency of action between the different levels, as is the case in Switzerland where there is a "Tripartite Commission" encompassing communes, cantons and the Federal level? Or is it preferable to increase the number of contracts between central government and the different interlocutor levels? In the case of Italy, the answer is clear. In a given territory which is a partner in many development assistance contracts, including supranational ones, setting up an intermediary local development body can prove beneficial with regard to the coherence of partnerships as a whole (the case of southern Italy). Including an ever growing number of stakeholders does of course help ensure the participation of all possible sources of innovation, but makes it difficult to respect efficiency criteria when determining common policy. As for France, it takes the view that responsibility for coordinating economic development rests with the regions, but without making them the leaders.

The duration of contracts

A lot of time is spent on initial co-ordination when setting up such mechanisms (*contrats de plan Etat Région* in France, territorial pacts and programme contracts in Italy, tripartite contracts in Canada, etc.). In Italy this is even seen as essential to guarantee the smooth execution of the contract, obviously because of the lasting quality of decision-making networks that share experience, references, objectives, etc. This is, however, very difficult to measure and is undermined by having a succession of contractual formats. Italy emphasises the need to set up clearer and more effective incentive mechanisms such as bonus systems and performance-related sanctions (inspired by the European performance reserve scheme).

Going beyond the administrative perimeters

Rather than merely viewing local economic development strategies as the output of relations between levels of administration, one can see in different member States that the competent regional perimeter, the partner in the new contracts, is itself the product of cooperative processes (as it is the case in Finland where regional councils are the result of inter-municipal partnership). Horizontal co-operation is therefore a prerequisite for intervention at the central level. This is the case with the "*contrats de pays*" for rural zones in France. Some countries adopt this approach specifically to urban development. By concluding multi-level urban partnerships, both central and local governments have agreed on a list of common tasks and on sharing the responsibility of fulfilling them (France and the agglomeration contracts; Canada and the Urban development agreements…). There are also a few recent types of metropolitan contracts (France, Switzerland…).

Recommendations

The comparative analysis brings us to six policy recommendations: transfer real responsibility to local authorities, strengthen the capacity of central government, focus on key programmes, ensure the transparency of the process, organise monitoring during the implementation of contracts, organise evaluation.

- *Transfer responsibilities from the central government to local authorities*: There is no need to review again here the justification for decentralisation of government, but we have to be clear on the meaning of decentralisation. It requires elected bodies at the sub-national and local levels, vested with autonomous rights. As regards contractual arrangements across levels of government, decentralisation is a precondition for their use. This shows the difference between management contracts, which are there to clarify the responsibilities within an organisation, and contracts which operate in a multi-level system of government.

- *Strengthen the capacity of central government*: Any large-scale devolution of responsibilities to sub-national levels that does not give central government the resources to keep the whole government system working might undermine overall coherence. Contractual arrangements across government levels may be a compromise, helping to reconcile the tendency towards decentralisation and the consistency of the policy-making system at central level. In this way, more responsibilities can be coupled with more co-operation. However, a basic condition for such a compromise is that there is a balanced distribution of resources of all kinds between central government and regional/local governments. Furthermore, contracts are not an alternative to classical instruments of government. On the contrary, the capacity to revert to using instruments of prerogative must remain an important resource in the central government's negotiating capability.

- *Focus contractual arrangements on key programmes*: The proliferation of contracts can dilute responsibilities and policies, and make coordination much more difficult. In this regard, it can help to have framework contracts. On the other hand, contracts whose content focuses on key issues will support the debate on those issues by giving it concrete application. Focusing contractual arrangements on key issues will also help to save administrative costs, facilitate the involvement of political assemblies in the policy-making process, and allow greater transparency.

- *Ensure transparency of contractual arrangements*: Transparency means both publicity and procedural requirements. Publicity should be ensured at all stages of the contractual process. It means documents must be made easily available to the public. Procedural requirements are more difficult to define and to fulfil. By contrast with planning documents, for which broad consultation and inquiry procedures are provided by law, as recently reinforced by EC directives, the legal regulations are rather weak where contractual arrangements are concerned, and the level of public participation is almost left to the discretion of local authorities. This is a paradox, considering how contractual arrangements come about, and the fact that they generally determine the content of public procedures that will be needed later to carry out a number of projects. Although it would be unjustified to introduce too many procedural obligations at the contractual negotiation stage, at least some part of the process should be open by law to public participation.

- *Organise monitoring*: This is a requirement especially for planning arrangements. When a contract is to last for several years, it is clear from the beginning that the implementation will not stop with the execution of the written contract. Mechanisms must be put in place so that the parties can share the burden of implementation, as well as the difficulties that arise and answers to them. An appropriate reporting system has to be established for this.

- *Organise evaluation from the beginning*: Everybody nowadays recognises the need for evaluation. But the results of evaluations are often disappointing, if not deceptive. Indeed, the quality of the evaluation is determined practically at the time of contract signature. The technical requirements of the evaluation have to be anticipated when formulating objectives and determining measures, and in setting up the reporting system. Collection of the information necessary for measurement has to be put in place from the very beginning.

In conclusion, contracts are complicated mechanisms. They primarily concern the vertical relationships between different levels of government. However, they cannot properly cover multiple sectors unless different ministries involved in regional and local development are able to coordinate their policies.

Organisation/reorganisation of the higher levels of government for regional development: a prerequisite

Several different models have emerged in OECD countries in order to improve co-ordination of territorial policies at national level. The spectrum of instruments ranges from bodies charged with co-ordinating the activities of sectoral ministries to full-fledged ministries with broad responsibilities and powers that encompass traditionally separate sectors.

The simplest and most common instrument is co-ordination through inter-ministerial committees and commissions. OECD governments all have numerous inter-ministerial committees to deal with cross-sectoral issues, among which there are generally co-ordinating bodies responsible for territorial policy domains such as regional policy, urban policy and rural development policy. Three characteristics of these co-ordinating bodies stand out: 1) formality/informality, 2) political level co-ordination, and 3) links with budget allocation mechanisms.

- Some co-ordinating structures are relatively informal, others are more structured. Austria, for example, has developed an informal approach that emphasises consensus building among different ministries, while Switzerland uses a more formal approach to policy co-ordination where ministries dealing with territorial development issues have to convene regularly in an inter-ministerial body.
- The task of managing co-ordination across ministries – i.e., chairing co-ordination bodies – is often a responsibility of the head of state, prime minister or cabinet. In the United States, the President's Cabinet is responsible for cross-sectoral co-ordination, in Mexico, the Presidency, in Ireland, the Office of the Taoiseach, in the UK, the Office of the Deputy Prime Minister, in Austria, the Federal Chancellery.
- The participation of finance/ treasury ministries and the link between the outcomes of co-ordination processes and budget allocation procedures is another important aspect.

Several countries augment cross-sectoral co-ordination mechanisms with the use of special units or agencies that provide planning and advisory support to help ensure policy coherence across sectors. In Norway, the Regional Development Unit of the Ministry of Local Government and Regional Development has been given responsibility to co-ordinate the regional dimension of the policies of other government departments, principally through inter-ministerial groups. In the UK, the Regional Co-ordination Unit – currently placed within the Office of the Deputy Prime Minister – was set up to implement cross-cutting initiatives and advise departments. In Japan, the National and Regional Planning Bureau within the Ministry of Land Infrastructure and Transport has developed a new perspective of territorial/ regional policy and provided a network for local authorities as well as other local actors. In France, the DATAR (*délégation à l'aménagement du territoire et à l'action régionale*) is an inter-ministerial body directly linked to the office of the Prime Minister (which coordinates national territorial policy and handles the planning contracts and the European Structural Funds) and receives the different ministries' information regarding their regional priorities and the strategic objectives identified by the regional prefects. DATAR also plays an important role in the allocation of funds: every year it collects budget requests from the regional prefects and allocates the budget to related ministries, and if necessary organises inter-ministerial meetings with the prefects and the ministries. When the ministries decide the amount of money they will distribute, they inform DATAR which in turn informs the prefects.

While co-ordinating bodies represent an important tool, decision-making power remains principally in the hands of the individual sectoral ministries that implement policies. As such, while the planning stage is more or less well integrated, implementation is potentially compartmentalized.

To overcome problems relating to sectoral implementation and in line with the increasing importance accorded to regional development policies, in some cases inter-ministerial co-ordination bodies have been empowered and given some responsibilities for implementation. The DATAR in France is an example of an inter-ministerial body that is charged with ensuring co-ordination but that also has a formal role in territorial development planning, decision-making and policy implementation. The Office of the Deputy Prime Minister in the UK has also evolved towards a broader and more active role than its original policy co-ordination remit. In Italy the Department for Development and Cohesion Policies within the Treasury Ministry has broad competence for programming and co-ordinating investments with particular reference to the Mezzogiorno regions.

An important additional function that these co-ordination bodies have adopted is as the interface with regional government in the field of economic development – allocating funding; setting the guidelines for drawing up regional strategies; advising on and authorising the strategies; and ensuring value-for-money.

The other approach to sectoral co-ordination is to overcome departmental boundaries by merging and combining departments. This is generally only a partial consolidation. For example:

- In 2001, Japan reorganised cabinet level ministries and agencies in order to establish more effective political leadership, improve transparency, streamline the central government, and improve efficiency. The new Ministry of Land, Infrastructure and Transport (MLIT) was created by amalgamating four ministries and agencies (the National Land Agency, the Hokkaido Development Agency, and the Ministries of Transport and Construction). Within the MLIT there has not been a radical reallocation of responsibilities and although MLIT was given specific regional development responsibilities, some important aspects of territorial policy are located in other line ministries (notably Agriculture and Economy, Trade and Industry).[14]

- The UK, similarly, created the Department of Environment, Transport and the Regions (DETR) which brings together several departments involved with spatial development. Responsibility for this large department rests with the Deputy Prime Minister, whose Office is also responsible for co-ordinating policy for the regions more generally. Nonetheless, the Department of Trade and Industry retains important regional economic development functions, and a range of departments and agencies combine to manage rural development policies.

Some countries have established regional development ministries, with broad responsibilities for different aspects of regional policy design and implementation. Good examples are provided by the former EU accession countries – Hungary and the Czech Republic, for example – in which regional development bodies were responsible for managing EU regional aids. As is discussed in the territorial review of the Czech Republic, the regional development ministry played a strong role in the allocation of EU funding, but its influence appears to be waning in the post-accession period. In the evolving context of regional development, it appears that there is a slow but progressive erosion of its initial competencies, although the MRD is the guarantor of the use of pre-accession and structural funds, jointly with the Ministry of Finance. Certain recent transfers of responsibilities and the creation of numerous state agencies with regional offices illustrate this. The management of SME support programmes in regions (most of which are administered by the Czech Moravian Guarantee and Development Bank) is no longer under the responsibility of the MRD[15] but of the Ministry of Industry and Trade (MIT), which finances these.

Finally, a completely different approach was taken in Canada where, in 1986 the federal regional policy administration was decentralised and four agencies located in the regions were created. The task of these agencies is to translate national priorities at the territorial level and represent regional and territorial interests in national programmes and policies. While at the broad level many of the activities undertaken by the Regional Agencies are similar (*e.g.* a focus on SMEs, reduced reliance on direct assistance to business, increased focus on innovation and communities), the programming varies from region to region in order to be responsive to local conditions and address specific gaps. The agencies are also members of an industry portfolio umbrella that includes other related departments and organisations thereby providing a mechanism for policy co-ordination that ensures a consistent federal approach to issues and national initiatives.

5. Horizontal co-ordination

Analysis will concern initially inter-municipal co-ordination before focusing on inter-regional and more particularly trans-border co-ordination.

Inter-municipal co-ordination

Inter-municipal co-ordination is on the agenda of many countries and is often a controversial issue. In some countries with a municipal structure that is highly fragmented, inter-municipal co-operation has seen tremendous growth, as in France, for instance, where 75% of the population has now been integrated under some kind of inter-municipal structure. The debate on inter-municipal co-operation is also intense in countries with a lower density of municipalities (as is the case for Mexico or Canada). Broadly, opinion on the inter-communal approach is divided. Offsetting the advantages it brings in terms of increasing the supply size of public services (which would enable improvements in both quality and quantity) are the extra costs of co-ordination and initial investment that increased size generates.[16]

There are two basic types of organisational form of inter-municipal co-ordination: municipal integration (by merger or by one municipality taking over another) and partnership-type arrangements, involving no more than a straightforward agreement on the joint supply of public services (covering one or more sectors) which can go as far as transferring powers to a joint body created specifically for that purpose (creation of an additional layer of local government or an institutional body such as an agency). This latter option amounts in a way to "re-centralising" at the intermediate level functions that previously used to be decentralised.

Why bring the municipalities together?

A number of theoretical arguments support the case for mergers

From the normative standpoint, putting municipalities together essentially provides the answer to the quest for greater economic efficiency (economies of scale, integration of spillovers) and fiscal performance. Economic theory suggests that the per capita cost of providing a level of public services follows an U-shaped curve, such that the cost of service provision declines with the size of population up to an "optimal" level before increasing beyond that point. Applying this theory to Japan, Hayashi determined that the optimal municipality size to obtain the lowest unit costs of public services is approximately 120 000 (based on 1990 figures). Using this figure as the benchmark, 80% of Japan's municipalities are under-populated and are not providing public services efficiently (Hayashi, 2002). The existence and magnitude of spillover effects from localised public policies clearly depend on the geographical extent of the relevant jurisdiction. One way to deal with such spillovers is to increase the size of the jurisdiction, thereby internalising all the benefits and costs. Regarding fiscal aspects, a unitary tax system and uniform tax rates allow greater fiscal equity within the amalgamated city, and amalgamation allows better policy coordination across the territory. Indeed, with fewer jurisdictions, firms may be less able to play off one jurisdiction against the others.

This search for economies of scale and for the integration of externalities means that inter-municipal mergers seem to be the mechanism most likely to enable the *communes* to grow in size. In functional models, governance structures are re-shaped to fit or to approximate to the functional economic area of the metropolitan region. Examples include the amalgamation of municipalities (Montreal, Halifax, and Toronto) and the creation of a metropolitan government (London and Stuttgart) (see Box 2.1). The functional model of metropolitan governance has some basic characteristics. First, it is based on governance at a functional economic area level. Second, it assumes that some decision-making power at the regional level is distinct and autonomous from either central, large regional or local government. Third, it is built around cross-sectoral competencies (i.e., not restricted to a specific sector or service) and competence in areas that have a metropolitan logic, such as transport, investment promotion, water supply, etc. The metropolitan model also holds out the promise of increasing the political power of the metropolitan region, *vis-à-vis* the central government and internationally.

... But there are difficulties

Defining the optimum size: The search for an optimal functional territory is futile because there is no one functional territory, but on the contrary, a multiplicity of functional territories depending upon the local public good or service under consideration. For instance, it is estimated in Denmark that 30 000 inhabitants is the optimal size as shown in an analysis of the costs of providing an effective local health system, an indicator used as a proxy for other local public services.

Problems of congestion linked to large size: Local public goods often show the characteristic of being "club goods" in the sense that the right to use them is limited to a finite group of people beyond which there is a risk of crowding. Beyond a certain number of users of the asset, the advantage that comes from others using it starts to diminish. A too-great supply of public goods can thus generate this sort of inefficiency.

Internal transaction costs linked to large size, and the issue of control: Economies of scale and of scope justify concentration. But the desire to better control local public choices, on the part of the voters as much as at the upstream government level, would seem to favour a smaller size while preventing, amongst other things, abuses of bureaucracy.

Problems of local competences: While some believe that amalgamation induces potential economies of scale, others, such as Kitchen (2002), argue that whether cost savings are realised depends largely on the quality of the

II. GOVERNANCE

> Box 2.1. **Metropolitan reform:
> the creation of the Greater London Authority**
>
> London is an unusual and perhaps atypical example to use in an analysis of metropolitan governance. Its metropolitan tier was abolished by central government decree and then re-created – in radically different form – fourteen years later. In 1999, the Greater London Authority Act was passed, and the GLA was set up in 2000. London has thus had four forms of governance in the past 40 years.
>
> The GLA consists of a directly elected Mayor and a separately elected Assembly, each elected for a term of four years. The GLA represents a new form of governance in Britain, with clear separation of powers between the directly elected Mayor and a small London Assembly of 25 members. The London Assembly must be consulted by the Mayor during the preparation of each of the GLA's strategies.
>
> The Assembly considers the budget for the GLA and for each of the four functional bodies and can over-rule the Mayor with a two-thirds majority. The Assembly scrutinises the exercise of the Mayor's functions and conducts investigations into London issues.
>
> The GLA has limited fiscal powers. It has no general revenue-raising powers: it cannot levy taxes nor issue bonds. It can raise income through an identifiable precept on the local authorities within the London area, but this is subject to the same powerful centralised control on taxing and spending that apply to all other British local authorities. As well as the precept, the other main sources of the GLA's income are government grants and the "congestion charge" on drivers in the central area, instituted in 2003. The GLA and its functional bodies spend around £5 billion per annum out of a total public sector budget of £45 billion. The 33 lower-tier authorities retain many powers and are responsible for most service delivery. The Mayor devises strategies, but he needs the boroughs, and other agencies, to implement them.
>
> *Source:* Dr. Mark Kleinman, Greater London Authority, quoted in OECD (2004) *Territorial Reviews: Mexico City.*

local public administration. Larger size requires new local capacity which takes time to be built.

Problems concerning local resources: Potential cost savings of amalgamation are sometimes obscured by the fact that new responsibilities have accompanied the creation of large merged cities without corresponding resources.

Problems arising from the abandonment of competition: For the Public Choice School institutional fragmentation and smallness are essential elements in maintaining competition and in permitting individual choice. In theory it is assumed that the factors are mobile and so competition between municipalities can have a positive impact on development inasmuch as it encourages municipalities to provide cost-effective services as well as greater diversity in the public services provided in a given area. The monopoly of merged governments in many services does not favour innovation or reductions in production costs. In fact, as far as the impact of competition is concerned, there are two competing schools. One central concern is that such competition leads to too little in the way of public outputs. It is argued that competition for new firms and jobs may lead to public budgets that are too small, and to overly lax environmental standards. Or, on the contrary, if those budgets are financed through central government grants, the competition across municipalities could lead to excessive spending. By contrast another thrust aims at the beneficial effects of competition as a disciplining force that restrains tendencies in the public sector towards excessive spending and other forms of fiscal misbehaviour. "One's view of the role of intergovernmental competition clearly depends on how one views the operation of the public sector more generally!" (Oates, 1999).

What do we see in practice?

Diverse "management" strategies of the effects of municipal fragmentation have developed over decades and in different countries. First of all municipal consolidation was at the heart of the debate. The reduction in the number of local municipalities has often been viewed as essential for the reform of decentralised institutions. Thus, some countries have made severe cuts in the number of local municipalities; operations which often went hand-in-hand with the introduction (or strengthening) of a regional or supra-municipal tier of government.

Municipal consolidation has been and remains an important element of most national programmes. Relatively speaking, the Scandinavian countries (Denmark, Norway, Sweden), along with the United Kingdom, are those in which municipal consolidation was pursued to the furthest extent, implemented with determination, steadfastness and authority. This was typically combined with public sector decentralisation within the local territorial bodies. Australia and New Zealand took over this policy in the 1990s, but with more mixed results (Sancton, 2000). Other countries have still not adopted this approach (or just to a very limited extent), for example Switzerland, France, Spain and the United States. In some federal countries, such as Canada and Germany, this policy is applied to very different degrees depending on the individual states (provinces, Länder) or on whether the context is urban or rural.

One can observe that economic efficiency is the main reason given for mergers in Denmark, Canada, Korea and Japan. Denmark considers that merely setting up co-operative arrangements is insufficient and, as has already happened in the past, wishes to increase pressure on communes to merge. However, most countries are of the opinion that the theoretical indicator of optimum size faces the problem of the variety of possible outcomes depending on the service in question, and in particular that trying to oblige municipalities to come together does not work. Some countries which adopted this type of policy in the past, such as the Netherlands, today consider that only one form is possible: that of voluntary agreements between communes, since this alone can guarantee a real co-operative sharing of objectives and communal costs (OECD, Symposium TDPC, 2004).

Regarding policy for inter-municipal co-ordination, the different degrees of "rapprochement" between communes may result simply from a policy adopted by neighbouring municipalities, from encouragement by the central authority or from a hierarchical decision taken by central government. Most countries support the second form of inter-communality (Czech Republic, France, Greece, Hungary, Italy, Mexico, Netherlands, Norway, Spain, Sweden...).

The main practical limits have to do with inertia in local identity (see Box 2.2). Municipal consolidation has always been (very) "popular" with senior civil servants and those working for the higher levels of government. Reluctance was expressed, on the other hand, essentially by local elected representatives. As for the inhabitants of these same municipalities, they often declined the invitation to merge with others because they feared losing a certain quality of life which they ascribed to "local identity". In fact, when the merger of municipalities is put to the popular vote (by referendum or otherwise), it has to be said that the result is almost always a refusal, even in the case of "watered-down" arrangements such as town-county consolidations in the United States. What is more, merged municipal structures seem less democratic than independent municipalities, because the distance increases between local authorities and citizens, resulting in lack of control over elected representatives. Finally, it is sometimes necessary to look to history for explanations of the local identity's strength. Institutional fragmentation thus becomes very difficult to reduce, as is illustrated by the "municipal demographic explosion" in the Czech Republic in reaction to the amalgamation imposed by the communist government.

Practicability and suitability of inter-municipal co-operation for economic development policies

Faced with these obstacles cooperative agreements appear like a workable second best. Inter-municipal co-operation has an advantage over mergers as it allows a diversification of the pooling of resources and of

> **Box 2.2. Illustrations of reticence with regard to inter-municipal mergers**
>
> **The case of Switzerland**
>
> Switzerland is interesting on more than one count. It is different from most European countries (except for France) in that the number of its communes remains stable. There are many local municipalities (over 2 300), generally with few inhabitants. In this federal country, municipal bodies are answerable to the federated states (cantons) and form an integral part of the constitutional framework in a country characterised by a tradition of direct democracy and consensus. Consolidating them is therefore a difficult, indeed almost impossible task. That said, the local political context in Switzerland is changing. In recent years, there has been a large increase in the tasks devolved to communes. This means in practice that communal tasks have become more numerous and complicated and that there has been an increase in interdependence. At the same time, the financial situation of communes is worsening whereas the demands and expectations of their inhabitants are increasing. Since the merger of municipalities can only be a last resort as a solution to this problem, there has been a sharp increase in inter-communal co-operation in recent years: except for the smallest and very rural communes (fewer than 250 people), nearly two-thirds have increased their participation in associations of communes in recent years (Steiner, 2003).
>
> **Other examples**
>
> Less than two years after its introduction, amalgamation in Montreal was already being questioned. The citizens' movement in favour of the detachment of their former municipality had gained new strength following the April 2003 election of a new government. The reasons for disamalgamation were both political (increased distance from decision-making centres), fiscal (lack of an economy inherent in the amalgamation and unfair redistribution of fiscal resources) and social (to preserve communities and identities). A referendum was held in June 2004 and 15 former municipalities decided to separate from the new city. Other attempts to introduce metropolitan governments by merging municipalities in Amsterdam and Rotterdam were rejected by referenda (more than 90% of Rotterdam's residents voted against).

partnerships, taking account of the multiplicity of the problems involved. Thus, the areas that provide different local public services can be respected and at the same time, the needs and preferences of local inhabitants can be better taken into account. Taking account of spillovers onto other jurisdictions can lead to the supply of local public goods being the product of a "bargaining process in which jurisdictions can swap externalities and establish their local public goods cooperatively" (Jehiel, 1997). There is a kind of "neither/nor" argument which sustains the use of co-operative modes: neither merger, nor competition. It is possible to take advantage of existing structures without recourse to heavy institutional forms through co-operation between local authorities as a substitute for amalgamation or metropolitan government, while voluntary co-operation between public authorities can meet the legitimate needs of the population that one town alone may not be able to satisfy. A related argument is that a municipal merger is unnecessary from the perspective of public service provision because there are many other means by which to achieve economies of scale (many of them involving joint production and provision of public services by partner municipalities, but also by the private sector, as described below).

Inter-municipal co-operation also covers very different situations depending on the context in which it is introduced and the goals pursued. Generally speaking, it takes the form of a pooling of resources (budgetary, human, infrastructure) in order to improve local public services falling within the jurisdiction of the member municipalities. All sectors of municipal activity can be the subject of co-operation agreements. It should, however, be noted that the list of municipal powers varies considerably across countries (see Box 2.3 on the US case).

As administrative boundaries do not necessarily coincide with areas that are relevant economically, municipalities can co-operate with the aim of

---

Box 2.3. **The US case**

In the United States since the mid 1950s, there has been a significant increase in Councils of Governments (COGs) and other forms of co-operation agreements for the planning, financing and production of local public services. By way of example, in the mid 1990s, the State of Connecticut alone counted more than 900 inter-municipal co-operation agreements (Berman, 2003). Thus, in the 1997 census, there were almost as many mono-functional agencies (special – purpose authorities, 34 683) as municipalities (multi-purpose governments, 36 001). Moreover, between 1992 and 1997, the number of special-purpose authorities rose rapidly (+9.9%). During this period, the number of such authorities increased in 43 out of the 50 States, in some cases in spectacular fashion (Wisconsin +84.6%, New Mexico +462.9%). In short, in the United States in general and metropolitan areas in particular, territorial organisation is constantly evolving and voluntary co-operation is being preferred to imposed solutions such as the merger of municipalities or the annexation of territories.

playing a more effective role in local economic development through exchanging information, sharing responsibility for certain investments, the joint production of knowledge, territorial labelling and marketing schemes to differentiate themselves from other areas, etc. This has led to the creation of metropolitan agencies, as in Montreal for instance, responsible for the planning and co-ordination of economic development. This issue is not exclusive to urban regions. In rural areas, the European LEADER[17] programme warrants mention. In intermediate regions, inter-municipal co-operation often takes the form of city networks (Emilia-Romagna), sometimes featuring the creation of innovative structures (Consortia of cities in the Valencia Region of Spain), with the aim of increasing the region's visibility and helping to make local enterprises more competitive.[18] These co-operative mechanisms, which lead to the creation of new institutional territories within the perimeters of social-economic areas and are adapted to territorial development strategies, are particularly evident in the concept of micro-regions (see Box 2.4).

As is clearly shown in Part I, the promotion of clusters and the local diffusion of innovations above all concern the local labour markets, meaning that there is no reason for the administrative boundaries to be exactly the same as those of the municipalities. The overlapping of responsibilities on this issue does not necessary hamper its good functioning and can, on the contrary, be a good support to joint strategies in the municipalities concerned. The same applies to tax rivalry, sometimes fictive, which has an influence on the localization strategies of companies. Finally, combining competencies rather than confronting them serves as a good support for innovation policies. Canada referred to the case of purely voluntary co-operation by communes which were *a priori* in competition with one another, which led to the setting up of an effective local system for innovation. Not only were the Province or Federal State not involved, but the successful outcome encouraged them rather to reduce the subsidies given to the territory in question (source: Symposium of TDPC, June 2004).

Therefore, following closely on from the "subsidiarity" principle, inter-municipal co-operation has the advantage over mergers or a strict institutional fragmentation, of proposing greater flexibility as regards determining the most appropriate territorial scale. In recent reforms in France aimed at aligning the administrative and socio-economic perimeters, the territory can even be the result of co-operation between municipalities. In practice, plans for a district ("pays") can arise out of agreement between the local authorities, and then gain recognition from central government. Inter-communalities are a key part of the machinery, as is seen from the case of the state – regional plan contracts of the last generation. The territorial arm that accounts for 25% of the budgets no longer falls under the responsibility of

Box 2.4. **An illustration of place-based policy in rural areas: The micro-regions**

A way to conceptualise the new vision of local development is what is called in many countries a micro-region, that is to say an association of municipalities aiming to achieve common development goals. They involve voluntary associations of local governments, groups of citizens and community participation. These actors are redrawing the boundaries of their territory, based on factors such as natural endowments, common identity, or shared economic characteristics. Micro-regions across OECD countries present three major features. Firstly, local actors develop their proper strategies to capitalise on their own assets. Secondly, they function as sources of information for central and regional governments. Thirdly, leadership in this kind of partnership is not the exclusive competence of elected authorities but can be assumed by groups of entrepreneurs or civil society organisations aiming to contribute to the definition and implementation of local development strategies and projects.

Support from the Government can consist in providing an adequate legal framework, as well as financial incentives such as in France, Italy and Canada. In other cases, "managed inclusion" of local authorities can help build associations based on the concept of "natural area of development", regardless of administrative borders. Such is the situation in Ireland where 34 LEADER Local Action Groups (LAGs), operating as Area-Based Partnerships manage a wide range of development projects (entrepreneurial, educational, social inclusion, employment and training, village renewal, cultural heritage and environmental preservation) without substituting the County's Development Boards.[19]

The size of the territory and number of co-operating municipalities are also variable and necessarily linked to population density. The territory of Matawinie, in Quebec (45 000 inhabitants), covers an area of 10 600 km^2 with only 15 municipalities, whereas the size of the Micro-region of Moravska Trebova-Jevicko in the Czech Republic is only 400 km^2, for a population of close to 28 000 people, distributed over 33 municipalities ranging from 36 inhabitants to 11 662 in 2001. In Mexico, total population in a micro-region can vary from 16 000 in the Micro-region "Sierra Gorda" in the State of Queretaro, to 122 000 inhabitants in the Micro-region "Sierra Norte" in the central state of Puebla. In some cases, the critical mass necessary to articulate a specific bottom-up initiative can be even higher. In the United States, a central Iowa project (pharmaceutical/nutraceutical plant production) involves 23 counties, with a population close to 480 000. However, currently only 72 farm families, playing the role of local leaders, are engaged in this up-scaling initiative (Mortensen, 2002).

representatives of the different ministries concerned but under that of the chairmen of the inter-municipalities of the region.

Diverse forms of co-operation

Variety of legal forms: The forms of co-operation between local authorities may range from simple "areas of co-operation" (like Spain's *comarcas*) to associations (like the *mancomunidades de municipios* in Spain, associations in Portugal, *communautés de communes* in France or the *unioni di comuni* in Italy) or the creation of "syndicates" as is the case in the Netherlands. In Luxembourg (with the approval of the Minister for the Interior) they may involve agreements that include both public and private entities working for the joint interests of the communes concerned. They may even result in the creation of inter-municipal co-operative authorities as in Finland, which has radicalised this concept to some extent, since the "region" as a territorial unit is based there on municipal co-operation (the regions were created starting in the early 1990s). In the Finnish system, regional autonomy was thus established "from the bottom up", with the result that, legally, the regions have the status of ordinary inter-municipal authorities.

Variety of economic types: Inter-municipal co-operation may be "functional", in which case the local authorities concerned will share the provision of specific public services, usually through establishments that are responsible for this undertaking, such as Germany's *Stadtwerke*, set up under the legislation of the Länder which requires all municipalities to merge their service provision units into one local public company (which in half the cases is a prelude to privatisation of the merged establishment) and is applicable to transport, drinking water, waste and sanitation, etc. Sometimes agreements lead to the initiation of a sort of trade exchange between neighbouring towns. The supply of public services is concentrated in some jurisdictions, which receive compensation from other jurisdictions benefiting from the services. This approach has been implemented is Switzerland, in particular in the area of hospital care services (more at an inter-cantonal level than an inter-municipal one) (Joumard and Kongsrud, 2003). On the other hand, inter-municipal arrangements can be geared towards more strategic local development missions and then cover a much wider field of action, sometimes supported by multi-sectoral agencies (especially in metropolitan areas).

Variety of geographical types: While inter-municipal co-operation is not a specifically rural or a specifically urban phenomenon, the distinction is significant. This is borne out by the division of inter-municipal structures into three types in France: the *communautés des communes*; the *communautés d'agglomération* (areas with a population of over 50 000); and, the *communautés urbaines* that can be set up only when the population exceeds the

500 000 mark. Evidence shows that the most extreme form of coming together (merger) only makes sense where the zones or municipalities are very close to each other geographically. There are still some agreements for the joint provision of public services that cannot be set up between rural communes at a great distance from each other. What may be considered appropriate policy for urban areas may not help much in dispersed rural communities where the delivery of high quality public services is an important tool used for regional development objectives (*e.g.* Norway). The case of the Canadian Province of Quebec also illustrates the importance of developing differentiated policies for urban and rural areas. In the course of its municipal reform, from 1999 to 2002, the provincial government was highly aware of the fact that heavily urbanised areas, rural areas and mixed urban/rural areas each required their own special strategy. So the preference went to consolidating municipalities in urban and metropolitan areas, strengthening the intermediate regional structure in rural areas, and stepping up inter-municipal co-operation in mixed rural/urban areas. This differentiating strategy aims to take into account the fact that these three types of municipal environments have different skills and above all utilise these skills in different ways, as is observed in the case of intermediate regions (see Box 2.5).

Assessment

Results of evaluations of inter communal policies are rare: a few studies have been carried out in Switzerland and the United States, but, paradoxically, hardly any in France, where it is a major tool of regional policy. The main benefits noted do not really include a reduction in the cost of delivering public services (Steiner, 2003 for the case of Switzerland; Moiso A. and Uusitalo R. (2003) for the case of Finland). An obvious advantage, on the other hand, is that local decision-makers enhance their skills as a result of sharing knowledge and of having to deal with bigger problems than those which a single commune has to face.

On this type of agreement, the effect of joining efforts for providing multi-services appears to produce significant economies of scope. On this subject, a pioneering analysis by Kathryn A. Foster (1997) of the situation in the United States showed that, overall, it is more costly to have local public services provided by specialised agencies rather than multi-purpose municipal governments and that this trend increases over time.

Neither academic research nor evaluations made by public or para-public bodies have shown that merging municipalities leads to economies of scale in all, or even most, cases (Sancton, 2000; Keating, 1995). Today, it is widely thought that the main advantages are not to be found in this sphere, but rather in a range of other values relating to community life and equity. In particular, in countries which have embarked on a significant decentralisation

Box 2.5. **Inter-municipal co-operation in intermediate regions**

Rationale: Lack of co-operation is a major problem of governance in intermediate regions, both in the private sector and between governmental jurisdictions. Competitiveness now depends on the quality of manufactured goods, on design and technological innovation. Every small or medium-sized city acting alone cannot provide all of the necessary human and material resources required for the development of the business sector. In this respect, it is essential to improve inter-city industrial networking policies and regional co-operation. Small and medium-sized towns will then be able to offer facilities and services that they could never afford on their own. This co-operative approach makes possible supporting the critical mass necessary for intermediate regions to gain a higher economic profile domestically and internationally. Networking of cities is optimised when it goes together with a process of specialisation of cities, whether in niche market products, through local industrial districts, or in industries based on tourism and natural and cultural amenities.

Examples: Regional networks of small and medium-sized towns and cities are a still modest but growing phenomenon in OECD areas.

One excellent example is the region of Emilia Romagna in northeastern Italy. Widely recognised for its industrial districts, Emilia Romagna is economically a high-performing intermediate region. It has registered an employment growth rate of 4.2% between 1995 and 1999 and a Gross Domestic Product (GDP) growth rate of about 4.5%. The region is characterised by an important cultural industry of festivals, attractions, and arts. Policymakers have encouraged the networking of the small and medium sized-towns coupled with a specialisation of each city in specific aspects of culture and the arts. This process of networking and specialisation was first borne from independent initiatives by local private entrepreneurs. Aware that these actions could help enhance cultural amenities, promote employment, and boost tourism, regional public authorities also supported the process but in an informal way.

Another interesting economic co-operation initiative, which has taken a more formal framework, concerns the Central Comarcas Valencianas (CCV), an intermediate region located in the central eastern part of Spain, comprising 155 separate municipalities in two different provinces. The CCV intermediate region has an important manufacturing sector specialising in textiles, clothing, and toys, organised in classical industrial cluster structure and highly oriented toward production for export. The public and private sectors have decided to work together in promoting new regional economic

II. GOVERNANCE

> Box 2.5. **Inter-municipal co-operation
> in intermediate regions** *(cont.)*
>
> and industrial policies. To pursue this agenda, they formed in 1999 the Consortium of Cities of the Valencian Central Districts. Its main purpose is to generate co-operation in overcoming the relative political marginalisation of the smaller industrial communities from the major metropolitan areas of the region, the cities of Valencia and Alicante, and to create a critical mass enabling the region to address strategically the new economic dynamics brought about by the ongoing process of economic globalisation.
>
> In France, the *réseaux de villes* (network of cities), is a contractual public/private partnership with associated representatives from the business sector, different local administrative entities, and the central government. These French city networks are neither political bodies nor institutions. Generally speaking, medium-sized cities join together in order to share costs and risks with a view to achieving complementarities and improving administrative procedures. The organisations that take part in the city networks collaborate on strategic planning, public-private partnerships, and joint development projects. Co-operation covers a wide range of issues including promoting tourism and culture, improving transportation, business marketing, environmental enhancement, and investing in new information and communications technologies.

process, consolidation is said to bring further benefits. Thus, because they shoulder a larger number of responsibilities, consolidated municipalities are thought to aid the revitalisation of democracy said to be needed, if not urgently, in our political systems.

One explanation given for the difficulty in showing a clear increase in efficiency brought about by the development of inter-municipalities is that the existing structures are becoming more and more complex. Thus in France, it is generally observed that the increase in public inter-communal co-operation establishments (EPCI), which can vary greatly in size, can make the system of 36 600 communes more complicated. Even if inter-municipal co-operation is generally positively assessed, there are, nonetheless, some cases where co-operation is not real, where it has not worked, where bypass strategies have been employed or even attempts to reverse cooperative efforts (Gaxie, 1997). Such cases of co-operation need appropriate and transparent cost accounting in order to determine the "price" of the public service at a fair level, and to limit the risk of free riding behaviour for "too" public goods (non excludable at all) such as roads.

The presence and above all the increase in the number of inter-municipal agencies constitutes a threat to municipal autonomy; which also can potentially erode accountability, particularly as they cloud the transparency of democratic processes.[20] Co-operation may also lead to awkward situations, as is the case when municipalities join together for a number of their functions while remaining competitors as regards territorial attractiveness (mentioned by Spain with regard to rural areas, June 2004, Symposium of TDPC). In fact, according to different situations, the former government system adapts to new realities by multiplying its actions. As a result only precarious and complicated solutions are found.

One of the pitfalls of inter-municipal co-operation is that of political representation which, generally speaking, is indirect rather than direct. In practice, it is local municipalities or member communes who appoint representatives to the decision-making body (political and/or administrative). Serious consideration should be given to the democratic argument. Voices have also been raised in France claiming that the representatives of the "inter-communalities" should be elected by universal suffrage, the more so where "inter-community" in a metropolitan zone is concerned where the budgets for common activities are often even higher than those of the cities at the heart of these metropolitan areas.[21]

Regarding the available resources of the co-operative structure, it is important to note that direct powers of taxation are rare. The inter-municipal body depends, for its funding, on transfers from higher governments, on the one hand, and on contributions from member communes, on the other. As a rule, the result is a longer decision-making process, and reduced ability to adapt to changing situations, business conditions or technical developments.

Trends noted and policy issues

Despite these controversial results, countries which have actively pursued a policy of inter-communality tend to want to extend co-operation to a wider area than that involved in simple *rapprochements* between neighbouring communes. It is essentially the economic development goals of a whole territory (for example the *"pays"* in France) which motivate this type of approach. At the end of the day, the main factor distinguishing different forms of inter-communality is therefore the goal pursued: some "simply" aim to improve the supply of a number of day-to-day services, while others adopt a more dynamic approach, endeavouring to establish a strategic vision for the region. Some "multifunctional" forms of inter-communality, as in Hungary, fall somewhere between these two types. Certain features appear to greatly facilitate inter-communal co-operation, especially in adding a fiscal dimension to the institutional one (sharing taxes and/or harmonising local tax bases and rates).[22]

The need for responsible structures at intermediate levels

One of the major risks of the increase in inter-municipal co-operation agreements is that the general interest of the conurbation or region can be lost from view. As Berman (2003) notes: "Inter-local agreements on services or facility use, while saving money, do little to promote a general area-wide perspective or to solve area-wide problems." Moreover since associations, in responding to a given problem, are usually sectoral, the joint approach means that an overall vision is somewhat lost. That is why it is desirable to set up or strengthen intermediate structures which encourage co-operation.

The very notion of pooling and of inter-municipal co-operation takes on much greater significance wherever there are strong – supra-municipal or regional – intermediate, multipurpose structures, as most co-operation initiatives are or can be part of a local community approach that is open to policy debate. The most common approach would be metropolitan associations of local municipalities at regional or sub-regional levels, where implementation and boundaries are decided on by higher levels of government. The introduction of such an intermediate level of government (supra-municipal or other level) plays an active role in structuring municipal co-operation. These formulas, typically with opt-in, opt-out possibilities, contribute to flexibility of the experiment by allowing for a step-by-step inter-municipal co-operation according to local circumstances and culture. They provide a driving force toward developing and intensifying co-operation among all or part of the municipalities in an area. Intermediate structures, like conferring responsibilities to an intermediate level (such as the regional level) for regional policy on inter municipalities, lends cohesion to the policies pursued in a given region, to the exchange of good practices, the bringing together of a greater variety of players in regional development projects, and thus to the creation of more favourable conditions for constructive innovation to emerge. This is the meaning to be given to the new French territorial structures (the districts [*pays*]) which, even though their responsibilities still seem ill-defined, were conceived of as "inter-inter- municipalities".

There are different examples to illustrate the variety of forms these intermediate inter municipal structures can take (see Box 2.6).

Consistency with the national governance system

In Helsinki, as elsewhere in Finland, a culture of co-operation between municipalities in the agglomeration is part of the broader organisation of central government and the public sector (Haila and Le Galès, 2002). Among the key factors for success for inter-municipal co-operation, voluntary commitment is important as well as institutional customs and the experience of elected officials. So this is first and foremost a process involving local and

> **Box 2.6. Examples of intermediate levels for co-ordinating inter-municipality agreements**
>
> In some United States conurbations, fields such as infrastructure management and funding, recreational facilities and activities, sport, culture and tourism have been identified as offering the potential for more co-operation throughout the metropolitan area. The latest example is that of the Allegheny Regional Asset District (ARAD, core city Pittsburgh) in Pennsylvania. In this County a tax formula was introduced which the legislator and local players saw as a means of simultaneously resolving, at least partly, two separate issues: *i)* the funding of infrastructure and/or activities on a supra-municipal or even regional scale; *ii)* the need to restore greater tax equity across local municipalities and alleviate the local tax burden for the largest taxpayers. By and large, the scheme reflects a determination to give the region better regional governance, without interfering with municipal arrangements, which are particularly fragmented. This formula, inspired by a measure introduced in Denver, Colorado, is a 1% sales tax levied by the State in accordance with the usual sales-tax rules in Pennsylvania, but all of the revenue goes to the region. The revenue is split into two equal parts, the first going to an independent body, the Allegheny Regional Asset District (ARAD), a single-purpose agency with a mandate to grant annual subsidies for infrastructure and recreational/tourism activities with a regional impact, in particular civic and cultural/recreational facilities, libraries, parks and stadiums; the second is divided up between the county and the 128 municipalities it covers. This experiment is now recognised to have made a significant contribution in two areas, in that it has alleviated tension between the core city and the suburbs regarding the specification, implantation, funding and management of regional-scale infrastructure, and secondly, it has created the potential to strengthen municipal co-operation throughout the metropolitan area, thereby generating a major reform of Allegheny County's policy structures and missions in 2002.
>
> The "county regional municipalities" (*municipalités régionales de comté*, or MRCs) in the province of Quebec (Canada) are another interesting example, showing how much momentum can be gained from an intermediate entity of this kind in rural areas. Set up between 1980 and 1982, MRCs are federations of local municipalities that exercise some mandatory and some optional powers on behalf of their members. The list of these has been growing by the year, particularly since the municipal reform in 2000/2001. There is evidence here that several MRCs – because of the territorial framework they create and the momentum they give – have played a decisive role in the emergence and shaping of inter-municipal clusters in fields that may or may not necessarily correspond to MRC policy areas (*e.g.* economic and tourism industry development, leisure facilities such as cycle-paths, and selective household waste collection) (Collin *et al.*, 1998).

> Box 2.6. **Examples of intermediate levels for co-ordinating inter-municipality agreements** (cont.)
>
> The experience of regional districts in the Canadian Province of British Columbia is often cited as an example. The flexibility of the intermediate model adopted there, in particular the Greater Vancouver Regional District (GVRD), is viewed by many academics as a very positive feature. The novelty of the GVRD lies primarily in its approach to metropolitan management. The municipalities belonging to it are free to *opt out* on some issues. Conversely, municipalities located outside the GVRD area, which is roughly synonymous with the Vancouver Census Metropolitan Area, may *opt in* to the GVRD or any of the agencies it heads.
>
> In Switzerland for some years now, the Federal Office for Territorial Development has been initiating and providing technical and financial backing for an urban policy based on co-operation in model projects on agglomerations to promote the emergence of a territorial framework of sustained co-operation and planning between municipalities.
>
> A similar form of co-operation is found in the Berlin-Brandenburg area of Germany, now that the Federal State of Brandenburg has set up an Urban Forum, whose achievements include the creation of an association representing the interests of Regional Development Centres, with a view to institutionalising a joint political arena and co-operation between local authorities, at least in the field of planning (Arndt *et al.*, 2000).

regional stakeholders. This review of the experiments, however, shows that the process cannot gain momentum, or fully succeed, if it is not part of a clearly enunciated and demanding government strategy, at both the institutional and fiscal level. A clear stance by central government has a more decisive influence than any of the policy areas addressed here can have on their own. Inter-municipal co-operation is a process which should form part of a more general reflection about the role of the public sector. This questioning must focus on re-assignment of responsibilities (following the "subsidiarity" principle) and on promoting more effective mechanisms to ensure democracy.

Cross border governance: a special case in horizontal co-operation

Interest in mechanisms for managing cross-border reigons is the result of two distinct international trends: *first*, supra-national integration is reducing trade barriers between countries, and *second*, decentralisation is putting more power into the hands of subnational governments. Both trends increase the feasibility and potential benefits of collaboration across the border.

Cross-border regions typically suffer from handicaps that make the challenge of increasing competitiveness greater than in a single country region. For example, cross-border regions generally suffer from fragmentation – of markets, of the labour force and of institutions. The border, even if completely or relatively open, usually constitutes a significant rupture of the natural or optimal delimitation of the area's economic space. Often, border regions feel the friction created by diverging fiscal or labour market regulations and some try to circumvent this friction through intensified cross-border co-operation. This friction decreases the competitiveness of the region as a whole and of its constituent parts. Similar points can be made about the sub-optimal diffusion of technology, co-operation among enterprises, social capital development, and allocation of labour and infrastructure in a cross-border region. The creation of a functioning cross-border region where these weaknesses are addressed and complementarities are maximised promises significant benefits for the participating regions.

Developing a successful cross-border region implies moving progressively to a higher degree of integration.[23] A "higher degree of integration" can have an enormous range of manifestations, economic, social, cultural and institutional. In the economic sphere integration would normally be accompanied by, for example, increased trade between the two regions, an increasing number of enterprises with contacts/co-operation agreements/joint ventures with enterprises on the other side, increasing harmonisation of the labour markets as evidenced by higher commuting flows and/or establishment of common employment services, with demonstrable increases in the number of cross-border job placements and training placements, and increases in the number and quality of cross-border research and development initiatives. Closer social and cultural relations could be reflected by increasing numbers of inhabitants on one side of the border speaking the language of the other. Greater integration of institutions could be evidenced by the establishment of joint planning committees and unified development plans. Finally, integration of physical infrastructure would result in, for example, reduction of travelling times between centres on different sides of the border and completion of "missing links" in the infrastructure system. These and many other outcomes would reflect an increasing level of integration between two regions separated by a border (European Commission [DG REGIO], 2000).

Yet, while the concept is clear, and many elements that would constitute a cross-border integration strategy are obvious, the practicalities of formulating and managing a coherent strategy are not. Cross-border integration is a kind of political-economic spectrum that runs from simple institutional co-operation all the way to functional economic interdependence implying joint decision making and resource sharing. Within the same country, the latter is difficult legally and administratively; across national borders it is extremely complex. As a result, the process is inevitably gradual and somewhat piecemeal, and policy making tends to be an amalgam of the different economic, social and political aspirations of different actors that are linked more or less closely with the development of exchanges across a border. Because the interest in building a cross-border integrated region is not only a local issue, non-local actors are strongly involved and their interests are reflected in the formulation of policies and institutions to encourage cross border exchanges. The interest "matrix" is vertical as well as horizontal, national (even supra-national) as well as local, both public sector and private.

Cross-border governance can be defined as the establishment of and adherence to a set of incentives, norms and organisations that are set up to co-ordinate policy making in a region where the functional area of economic activities does not coincide with the geographical pattern of political jurisdictions. The mismatch between catchment areas and political jurisdictions leads to negative externalities and financial imbalances and can complicate coherent planning for region-wide infrastructures and network industries. The issue for policymakers is to find governance mechanisms, i.e. tools and incentives, that enable policy coherence in spatially and economically homogenous but politically fragmented areas.

The economic logic that drives efforts to build cross border co-operation is often explained in terms of relative transcation costs. On the one hand, there is the cost of policy non-coherence, and, on the other, there is the cost of adhering to and maintaining cross-border institutions and rules. The policy question is which governance rules best reduce or eliminate negative externalities, and which adapt the most smoothly to national frameworks. Cross-border frameworks and their ability to reach political objectives can be evaluated along four lines (in brackets the perceived economic transaction cost): 1) the nature and integrity of co-operation (social capital in the region); 2) the positioning strategies of the partners (costs and benefits of co-operation *versus* non-co-operation); 3) the contribution to organisational diversity (risk diminution and stability); and 4) the interaction between cross-border co-operation and other national, local and regional networks (transaction costs between institutions).

In Europe, cross-border issues, always important, have become more important with the wave of EU integration during the 1990s. Supranational integration made cross-border collaboration easier since it lowered the cost of interchange. Integration and cohesion are viewed as essential in maintaining an effective and internationally competitive European Union; as a result, border regions have become somewhat the darling of regional policy. As demand for cross-border governance has multiplied, so has the supply of governance and programmes sustaining it (see Box 2.7 for an example). The

> Box 2.7. **Cross-border governance: The examples of TriRhena and Öresund**
>
> During the last decade, cross-border initiatives have proliferated in OECD member countries. TriRhena on the Swiss-German-French border and Öresund on the Danish-Swedish border are among the most active cross-border regions in Europe.
>
> The Öresund Region, covering the cross-border area along the Öresund belt between Denmark and Sweden, established in 1994 the so-called "Öresund Committee", a broad platform for horizontal partnerships and formalised advice and information exchange. The Committee is composed of local and regional political bodies from both sides of the Sound and – which is quite exceptional for transnational regionalism – by the two national ministries as observers. There are no private actors in the Committee. Although elected local politicians represent the Committee, it does not act as a local or regional government but as a meeting place for the elaboration of public strategies on both sides of the border.
>
> Regio TriRhena is located right in the heart of Europe, representing parts of north-western Switzerland, southern Alsace (France) and southern Baden (Germany). Regional policy actors in 1995 created the Council of the Regio TriRhena, a 60-member council bringing together representatives of cities, municipalities, economic organisations, and universities that meet at least twice a year. Cross-border institutions, tri-national congresses and other initiatives enhance cross-border projects and initiatives by making information easily available. The TriRhena Council operates as an organ of co-operation parallel and complementary to the Upper Rhine Conference that represents a much bigger area.

European Union has started numerous programmes to foster cross-border collaboration such as the INTERREG programme, but also other programmes that intend to hoist the number of transnational networks and to increase the competitive edge of border regions. The European style of cross-border integration has often resulted in a multitude of organisations that cover many policy areas simultaneously by relatively complex governance structures.

Despite their ambitious declarations, cross-border governments in Europe have often failed to reach regional development objectives. The cost of co-ordination and common decision making often appears to outweigh expected benefits. It appears that horizontal partnerships are successful and sustainable only if they benefit both partners and the benefits are distributed more or less equally.[24] Effective collaboration fails in cases where both regions stand in strong competition or where a common endeavour benefits only one of the partners.[25] Particularly in the field of urban planning or fiscal co-ordination, local ambitions and strong competitive pressure have impeded most attempts at better co-ordinated cross-border regionalisation. In some cases, cross-border collaboration has hardly extended beyond the reach of EU sponsored INTERREG projects (Scott, 1999). Moreover, there remains a high degree of administrative complexity and public sector dominance on co-operation incentives. Europe's dense institutional and policy networks supporting cross-border co-operation have not automatically resulted in the establishment of new public-private alliances to address regional and local development issues (see Box 2.8). At its most successful, collaboration has worked mainly where public agencies have been strongly involved and had a direct say in project definition and implementation.

> **Box 2.8. Obstacles to cross border institution building: the starting point for Vienna-Bratislava**
>
> To establish regional cross-border institutions in the Vienna-Bratislava region appears relatively more difficult than in other cross-border regions. First, although both regions have a common history, the rigorous separation of the last 40 years has left the region with only a weak cross-border network. There has been no gradual evolution of cross-border institutions, like in the Swiss-French-German "TriRhena" region or the German-Belgian-Dutch "Euroregion". Second, unlike, *e.g.* in the Nordic countries, institutional differences between Austria and the Slovak Republic are quite significant, and, moreover, there are no supra-regional integration frameworks like the Council of the Nordic Ministers in place. Third, the Vienna-Bratislava region somewhat lacks a large infrastructure item to symbolise integration such as the bridge that links Southern Sweden to Eastern Denmark and acts as a symbol for "Öresund" integration. In Vienna-Bratislava, cross-border collaboration is starting from a low level and has to proceed in a very pragmatic way.

This differs somewhat from the pattern on the North American continent where governance structures tend to be more flexible, more oriented towards a few purposes, better able to react to specific problem situations and more driven by the private sector and local governments. North America's drive for regional integration is motivated much more by direct economic concerns rather than by a sense of a common "North American destiny" (see Box 2.9).

Cross-border co-operation has a very pragmatic appeal in North America. There is no broad policy platform for this co-operation and little national incentive for co-operation at the local level. It is not driven mainly by the idea

> **Box 2.9. The example of Cascadia**
>
> An example of a young but dynamic cross-border region in North America is Cascadia at the western edge of the US-Canadian border. Cascadia is dominated by the Pacific Northwest Economic Region (PNWER), a public-private partnership which was founded in 1991 among legislators, governments and businesses of five American states – Washington, Oregon, Idaho, Montana and Alaska – and three Canadian provinces/territories – British Columbia, Alberta and the Yukon. Over two decades, it has grown into a comprehensive institution that promotes regional economic development and competitiveness. PNWER has forged a unique collaboration between the public and private sector. PNWER has designated nine targeted sectors of business and industry that are strong within the PNWER jurisdictions and developed proactive working groups for each sector. Each working group is led by a legislative, public sector, and private sector co-chair. The working groups have initiated legislation, sponsored teleconferences, industry forums, and produced research papers.

of "overcoming borders" but rather by case-to-case problems, which for their efficient solution require selected action across the border. There is no lack of regional transnational problems such as water resource management (particularly in the case of Mexico-United States), environmental protection, public health and in more densely populated areas, fiscal and labour market regulation issues in cross-border commuting regions. The governance solutions follow the case-by-case approach: they are mostly carried out by single body associations such as Water Advisory Boards, Commissions on Environmental Co-operation and others.

Since NAFTA was signed, however, several organisations at the national level have emerged to promote cross-border interaction. For example, the North America Development Bank was made responsible for providing loans to projects on the US-Mexican border. This demonstrates, as has been the case in Europe, the importance that national policymakers put in local level cross-border initiatives as a means of reinforcing international agreements.

6. New actors in economic development strategies

Why cooperate with private actors?

Beyond the closer collaboration between central and local governments, or between local or regional authorities, there has been increasing acknowledgment that purely public intervention has its limits, and this has opened the way for greater co-operation between the public and the private sector. In fact, the involvement of private actors in the supply of so-called local public goods is nothing new (even if there has been a recent increase in the use of these methods in the fields of social welfare, environmental protection, etc.) and there are some who regard it as the key element in the definition of governance.[26] As long ago as 1974, Coase (Nobel prize 1991) relied on the example of lighthouses to expound the notion of the public good. The metaphor of the history of lighthouses and maritime signalling helps to understand that a public good does not necessarily have to be supplied by the government. Indeed, throughout the centuries, lighthouses have been built and managed by private investors, maritime corporations and associations from the public and private sectors. (Coase, 1974; 357-76).

The main normative advantage of PPPs is that they split the costs and risks of a project between the public and private sectors, particularly by tapping into the expertise and economies of scale in the private sector. However, beyond this advantage, the main issue is the shared will of the different actors to improve their living conditions and the economic development of the territory. The economic dynamics of the regions requires that all the actors at national, regional, and local level, from the public as well as the private sector, can be involved in decisions regarding their future. This enables private partners to share decision-making or even the implementation of existing services with the public authorities, either out of direct economic interest, as suppliers, or out of an indirect economic interest as users. In an economy that places a very high value on knowledge, regional development policy cannot afford to disregard the cognitive resources available. Public private partnerships (PPPs) therefore aim to enhance or provide an institutional framework for the involvement of firms, citizens and a variety of associations in local and regional economic development. Thus the key issue becomes not how to improve the efficiency of public spending, but more how to ensure that private governance of "public" activities can still function in the interests of society.

PPPs and regional competitiveness: three types of arrangements

- PPPs which are designed to enhance territorial competitiveness and therefore attempt to build, improve or promote the local and regional economy through interaction between public and private instruments for developing research, innovation and its diffusion at local level (where partnerships will primarily link public organisations and firms) (see Box 2.10). To this category can be added PPPs that aim to transform a natural amenity into a competitive asset. Such is the case in Sweden, in the region of Arjeplog, where the private sector has asked assistance from public authorities to bring into profit the economy of a remote area with very difficult climatic conditions. These conditions have made it possible to

Box 2.10. **PPPs for local innovation**

Support for innovation provided by clusters (or innovation ecosystems, districts, "pôles de compétences", etc.) consists of two types of public/private interaction.

The first is one in which firms located within a territory co-operate with public research and training institutions. Besides programmes aimed at involving industry in public research activities (either through the provision of funding or by identifying research targets), consideration must also be given to the bodies that draw up the technical and vocational training programmes offered at the territorial level and that include representatives of local industry. This type of partnership should not focus solely on the dissemination of research findings, but should also help to assist "receptive" firms (primarily SMEs) gain access to these unknown sources of competitiveness. An interesting initiative in this respect is due to be launched in the Midi-Pyrénées region in France. The aim is to make available a mature researcher one day a week to an SME (the SME will pay 50% of the daily salary of the researcher, with the remainder covered by public funds) to assist with the firm's technological watch and in identifying potential scientific partners.

In the second type of interaction, the public actor encourages partnerships between firms at the local level. This may be achieved by offering financial incentives to firms to co-operate and to join networks (Italy), through the training and provision of intermediaries (SEBRAE agents in Brazil, Brokers in Denmark and Business Links in the United Kingdom), through support for the creation of shared service centres (Emilia-Romagna and Lombardy regions in Italy), and through risk-sharing incentives to firms to support the creation of local start-ups. A heavy emphasis is also placed on organising venues where actors can meet, talk to each other and share in activities of not only a professional but also a social nature (organisation of regular cultural events associated with the location, organisation of sporting activities, clubs for managers involved in various cultural associations, etc.). In the United States, the involvement of the private sector in territorial development is one of the very criteria for granting subsidies by the Federal State. In order to receive such subsidies, local actors must form a network, propose projects that are coherent with the regional programme and are "market based", in the sense that leadership or the larger part of the capital invested is provided by the private sector. This is seen as essential if the assistance contributed by the central government is to lead to the creation of jobs.

These various options are aimed at building trust between actors on the basis of practical projects, at establishing a proper management system for the business network and, above all, at fostering a coherent vision to which managers from both the public and the private firms can subscribe.

- establish a "crash test" cluster in extreme conditions, attracting all the major automobile manufacturers (OECD Symposium, TDPC 2004).

- In some cases, and this was the earlier approach, PPPs are a means of finding other sources of funding for the provision of public services. The formal partnerships may include a wide range of distinct practices that can be traced to two major models. On the one hand, there are PPPs that have a purely contractual nature, in which the partnership between the public and the private sector is based solely on contractual links, and on the other hand PPPs with an institutional nature, involving co-operation between the public and the private sector within a distinct entity (source European Commission, green paper). These two normative types show differences in the remuneration of private actors and the public authority's capacity of control. However, they only concern one type of objective, which is assigned to the participation of the private actors: that of supplying one or several given public services. These partnerships are well developed and in particular have lead to extensive analysis from the point of view of competitive regulation and contractual methods linking the different partners. Still today, in many countries, most partnerships between local authorities and the private sector relate essentially to infrastructure supply (for schools, hospitals, etc., as is the case in Japan). PPPs are aimed at providing the infrastructure (in terms of network technology, housing, etc.) required for the local supply of public services (see Box 2.11). These agreements are based on a wide variety of contracts between local public actors and private firms, and may take the form of sub-contracting, concessions, the creation of mixed companies, agencies, etc. Depending on the circumstances, partnerships may be formed for a single targeted action or as a vehicle for longer-term co-operation between public and private actors.

- PPPs which are aimed at developing services of general economic interest that help local development, and which involve the active participation of civil society (i.e. the firms and user members of the public concerned) (see Box 2.12). Regional development projects are complex from the governance standpoint since most of the time they involve more public/public/private/private partnerships (PPPPs) than public/private ones (PPPs). Vertical agreements between different levels of government and/or horizontal agreements between municipalities and local public agencies are combined with relations with private actors.

The selection of the private partner

The European Commission, in order to improve the efficiency of the competition regulation concerning PPPs, has proposed a distinction between PPPs having a purely contractual nature, and PPPs with an institutional nature.[27]

> **Box 2.11. PPPs for the supply of local infrastructure***
>
> PPPs of this kind are traditionally divided into three types of models according to institutional format, the ways in which private partners are selected, the resources and input provided by the various partners, and lastly the way in which risks, and also benefits, are divided between the partners.
>
> *Local public enterprise:* an enterprise pursuing public goals of general economic interest and in which one or more local authorities hold at least 50% of the capital (or a genuine controlling share). In 2001, for example, 13 000 local enterprises of this type were reported in Europe. Their businesses covered all services of general interest to the economy (networks, transport, infrastructure, etc.). Examples include "limited companies" in Sweden, *Stadtwerke* in Germany and Austria, "communal firms" in Spain, "intercommunales" in Belgium, etc. Work of general economic interest is either mandated or sub-contracted to firms.
>
> *Mixed company:* in this model (which encompasses the above type of enterprise), transparency in the choice of private actor is an important issue. In Belgium, for example, the *Société de développement de la Région bruxelloise* issues competitive calls for tender in order to choose the most efficient private partner, thereby ensuring that the process is both competitive and transparent. French and Italian mixed companies tend to resemble this model.
>
> *Concession:* an arrangement whereby the public authority transfers the responsibility for funding (mostly provided by the private sector) to the private sector, with the risk borne entirely by the private operator, while benefits are shared between the parties. The Public Finance Initiative in the United Kingdom, designed to save on public funding, is one example of this type of agreement.
>
> These three definitions circumscribe the type of arrangements found in practice. It is important to note that in many cases the types of PPP encountered in practice are based on joint bodies that "institutionalise" the intermediation between partners (agencies, management committees, etc.)
>
> * These may include common infrastructures, facilitating educational exchange, tourism activities, environmental protection, and maintaining water resources, parks and natural reserves, as well as other local facilities and their cross-border use, where projects have flourished.

In the case of *contractual partnership*, the selection of the private partner could be based on an adapted procedure (defined for European countries by Directive 2004/18/C) commonly known as "competitive dialogue", which may apply when awarding particularly complex contracts. The competitive dialogue procedure is launched in cases where the authority is unable to define the technical means that would best satisfy its needs and objectives or

Box 2.12. **Participatory PPPs for "territorial projects"**

Involving private actors in regional strategy and planning seems to be increasingly widespread today. In the United Kingdom, for example, it is a characteristic of the recent PPP arrangements (especially in northern regions), where it is considered to be a prerequisite for strengthening the commitment of the various parties to shared objectives. In this type of partnership, the private sector actors are invited to participate in the definition of objectives and strategies with respect to local and regional policies. This could be an institutionalised form of participation as is the case with *Conseils économiques et sociaux régionaux* (regional economic and social councils) which represent the interests of enterprises and business associations in the planning contracts (*contrats de plan*) in France or the strong rules on participation in local development policy in Finland. In other cases, public-private interaction is more spontaneous.

The Sacramento Water Forum (an association made up of firms, federal agencies, local government, environmental protection associations) spent 5 years building a consensus to draw up, in 1999, an agreement on water management strategy and procedures in a semi-arid environment. This result, obtained after an initial context of tension, has prompted the regional government to reproduce this model of partnership-based decision-making in other domains. It has primarily been disseminated through "frontier actors", who, having been won over by this type of practice, have encouraged other groups, notably from industry, to take part in local programmes for sustainable development.

Another example is the QIM (Montreal International District)(an association made up of the federal government of Canada, the Montreal International District residents association (ARQIM), the city of Montreal, etc.) as part of a partnership-based project to promote the district which has involved residents not only in the decision-making phases but also in the financing of the project.

These examples reflect the important role played by time in creating a convergence between interests that are initially antagonistic, as well as the strong influence exerted by reputation in the concluding of agreements and the relevance of having a flexible structure for interaction (notably with regard to mutual learning processes). Such examples are legion. In most cases they are found in the areas of tax reform, education, environmental protection, approaches to economic development, transport, etc. In most cases it is practical necessity that lies behind efforts to work in co-operation with new networks of actors. Indeed, policy practice is often the first instance in which individuals sharing a specific space (regional or local) intentionally meet and interact.

in cases where it is objectively unable to define the legal and/or financial form of a project. This new procedure allows the contracting bodies to open a dialogue with candidates for the purpose of identifying solutions capable of meeting these needs. At the end of this dialogue, the candidates will be invited to submit their final tender on the basis of the solution or solutions identified in the course of the dialogue. Those tenders must contain all the elements required for the performance of the project. The authority must assess the tenders on the basis of the pre-stated award criteria. The competitive dialogue procedure will provide the necessary flexibility in discussions with candidates on all aspects of the contract during the set-up phase, while ensuring that these discussions are conducted in compliance with the principles of transparency and equality of treatment, especially the rules concerning state aid, frequently involved in case of territorial development and R&D.

By creating an *institutional partnership*, *e.g.* joint venture, the mixed entity has the task of ensuring the delivery of work or services for the benefit of the public. Direct co-operation between the public partner and the private partner with legal personality allows the public partner, through its participation as a shareholder and in the decision-making bodies of the joint entity, to retain a relatively high degree of control over how the projects go forward, which it can adapt over time as circumstances require. It also allows the public partner to develop its own experience of running the service in question, while having the support of a private partner. This kind of partnership is more and more frequently used in regional development for these reasons. The selection of a private partner called on to undertake such tasks while functioning as part of a mixed entity can not be based exclusively on the quality of its capital contribution or its experience, but should also take account of the features of its bid – the most economically advantageous – measured against the specific services to be provided.

Despite these rules and recent efforts to define them (in particular at the European level), results of the selection process are not homogenous. Some authorities practice tried and tested procedures, as in Liverpool, but other municipalities find themselves mired in disputes or fear of corruption, which paralyse the entire dynamic. For instance, this was the case in Prague for the building of a suitable ice hockey arena in time for the 2004 World Ice Hockey Championship.

Risks and recommendations

Two aspects of PPP arrangements must be capable of assessment: their performance in terms of the implementation of local development projects (improvement in the quality of public services, benefits produced in terms of employment, investment by private partners, etc.), and also their ability to put in place efficient co-operative structures making it possible to build up trust and shared references. Nonetheless, it is extremely difficult to gather data on these aspects, mostly due to the following problems:

- The distribution of responsibilities: even where contracts or protocols define the role of each partner as strictly as possible, the result can still be unclear. Where the partnership has been presented as a way of improving matters, it can become a source of confusion, diluting responsibilities and in the long term undermining credibility.
- The second problem comes from the unequal sharing of costs and benefits between the partners (for example, private partners generally fear that public authorities will treat them as instruments and control them).
- The third has to do with the search for windfall effects: some partners will only take part in " public production " for as long as it takes to derive the benefits without contributing to the costs that go with them. Follow-up in the provision of public services risks falling on the public actor if the private partner should default.
- The fourth problem is that private logic might overtake public logic, for example, where everything depends on the specific asset the subcontractor is asked to deploy, there is nothing to prevent the public authority from becoming the hostage of its own subcontractor. This type of locked in situation may also appear when one partner has a dominant position which can make regional development mono-functional (see Box on Logistic Centre Wolfsburg GmbH – Germany). Governments then find themselves obliged to serve the interests of individual actors first, in the hope that they will subsequently act in the common interest (by maintaining employment in the territory, by participating in the local market, etc.).

These principal-agent types of risk, argue for the involvement of a third party with powers. The idea of central or regional intermediation appears to be a more effective solution than merely having control agencies to ensure that certain rules are complied with, and also to ensure that there is enough incentive in terms of reputation derived from the possibility of repeating the process in other regions. Furthermore, this intermediation body can be given powers of sanction making the "threats" (penalties for non-performance) in the contractual mechanism real.

Information asymmetries are frequent where the dialogue between public and private sectors did not allow all the possibilities for collaboration to be identified at the outset. In recent years, some countries have developed centres of expertise, which have facilitated a common understanding and which offer the authorities their assistance in clearly identifying needs and expectations. In the Netherlands, communities of firms launched initiatives to develop similar information, playing the role of "sparring partner" for the local authorities. Also in that country, a centre of expertise has been set up with

Box 2.13. **Logistic Centre Wolfsburg GmbH – Germany**

The headquarters of the internationally operating global player in the transport sector, Volkswagen AG, have been located in the German region and city of Wolfburg since the company's foundation in the 30s. Interdependencies have always existed on economic development and regional planning and transport infrastructure between the city and the dominant regional company. Already, since the end of the 80s, the city and the company, as the most important actors in the region made an effort to establish a Logistics Centre (*Güterverkehrszentrum*: LC/GVZ), which connects the two transportation systems "railroad" and "highway" via a technical interface.

The GVZ Wolfsburg PPP is strategically embedded in the regional renewal concept "Auto Vision", which covers as main elements new measures of labour policy, a start up campus and tourist events ("Car City Wolfsburg"). This concept was developed and is managed by another public-private joint venture, the so-called "Wolfsburg AG". While this "framework company" is a 50:50 PPP, the majority of the shares of the GVZ joint venture is in private hands: VW AG and the city of Wolfsburg both hold 26% and an association of local logistics SME 48% of the shares.

The most important strategic and financial objectives of a GVZ-PPP-project were the following:

- To contribute to compensating staff reduction of the Volkswagen AG in the early 90s (app. 6 000 jobs between 1992 to 1994) due to the fostering of start ups in the regional logistics sector (industrial park) to establish an attractive regional transportation centre for VW AG, as dominant regional player, and other private and public actors in the transportation sector.

- Fund raising of public financial support (diverse EU Structure and Cohesion Funds via the state of Hesse: app. DM 4.75 m altogether), as the potential public and private partners were unable to invest the estimated DM 18 m for the first phase of construction.

- The integration of the Deutsche Bahn AG in the financial responsibility for the PPP investment, which should benefit long term from the reorganisation of the internal transportation of VW and in the region in aid of the railroad system.

- To reduce the traffic emission up to app. 15 to 20% as an explicit environmental objective.

Five years after the start of the GVZ Wolfsburg, the balance of the public and private partners is quite positive. The creation of approximately 1 500 new jobs was directly or indirectly influenced by the construction of the LC and the surrounding industrial park. There is sometimes slight criticism that the GVZ Wolfsburg and the public financial support are "tailor-made" for the Volkswagen AG as dominant player in the regional economy, while logistics SME (46% of the shares) bear the main economical and financial risk of the GVZ PPP.

central government backing, to act as intermediary and adviser in PPP relationships (see Box 2.14).

Finally, we should mention the risk that such local partnerships might be set up essentially for the benefit of large businesses, which would exclude drawing on the competences of local SMEs. In a world where globalisation affects all segments of the economy, the size of the proposed operations becomes a factor for competitiveness; and it can be seen that a growing number of regional development operations are becoming larger in size, more complex and with more specific expertise. Nonetheless, the involvement of mixed companies and local investors has to be evaluated with particular care, and their participation in PPP operations should be encouraged, because these actors seem, despite the potential for short-term disruption, to be the most motivated by regional development issues, as they are in urban development where the actors concerned are accustomed to taking major risks. It is important to insure that the size of the operations does not discourage some actors and that inequality in risk-taking does not lead to an increase in prices.

In the light of this, authorities have to intervene efficiently to ensure equal access to information. There is currently a market for PPP, but it is reserved to the larger actors, who alone are able to be present on the different regional and national markets. Now, the high stakes regionally and locally are such as to justify public funds being allocated to incite medium and small actors to participate, especially local ones.

Looking more towards the future, the risks vary depending on the economic success of the regions concerned: in rich areas, market forces may allow private/private partnerships to operate, involving risks in terms of the local supply of public services and of coherence with regional and national programmes. In areas in difficulty, on the other hand, it may prove difficult to motivate private actors to participate in local development projects, and effective incentives will be needed. However, it has been found that in disadvantaged urban areas, for example, those involved at an early stage can expect to make a good profit, but this is less certain for those coming after (Vermaylen, 2001).

7. Shared issues in co-operative governance instruments

The following describes three shared issues in multi-level governance.

The dual policy goal

In each of the institutional devices set up, there can be instrumental and/or relational outcomes.

- Instrumental outcomes: inter-municipal co-operation to improve the scale of supply of public services, PPPs to make use of private sector funding,

Box 2.14. **Expertise advice and comprehension between public and private sectors – The Netherlands**

The PPS knowledge centre from the Dutch Ministry of finances has worked for 4 years. It provides services to the various local authorities, mainly the municipalities, in order to create various types of infrastructures, especially when considerable investments are needed, and to address regional development projects. PPP is considered solely as an instrument for politics, there is no centre for debate or evaluation about operational orientations. The centre provides three services of advising and supporting, but does not substitute for managers:

- The identification of projects which can be run through PPP methodologies, the definition of the principal features, the selection of an appropriate methodology.
- Assistance to achieve the objectives according to the agenda and the methodologies which are set up.
- Good communication on the results which are reached, in order to allow an improved partnership, particularly regarding the confidence of the private sector.

The OPS foundation (*Onderneming voor partnership in stadvernieuwing*) established in 1998; participants in the OPS are companies and organisations that have economic interests in the urban renewal neighbourhoods. The OPS operates from this economic perspective: "It is important to create better investment conditions and to induce more commercial investments in vulnerable areas. Good business opportunities and a strong local social-economic climate go hand in hand."

The key-objectives are as follows:

- Adding economic perspective to urban renewal areas.
- Providing a platform for combining and exchanging knowledge and expertise in urban renewal.
- Promoting interests through available knowledge and expertise in the business community.

The working method is based on:

- stimulation, information and advice for local parties such as city councils, businesses, building corporations, investors, Government authorities;
- playing the role of sparring partner in concrete urban renewal project,
- being a centre for discussion and exchange of know-how.

devolution of management to local public authorities rather than of strategic responsibility.

- Relational outcomes: intended to ensure that co-operative practices produce a genuine improvement in knowledge and possibilities for innovation based on the variety of stakeholders involved in determining local strategies. This relational objective means trying to obtain better relations among the parties, increased trust, increased social capital, empowerment of the community concerned.

Both instrumental and relational outcomes must be taken into account when evaluating a co-operative process, and are partially connected. If a co-operative process fails on a substantive ground (it does not produce any sound solution or ends up in a general impasse), it will hardly generate better relations among the participants. Indeed it will be likely to spread resentment, frustration and mistrust. But the two aspects are not always so tightly connected. A co-operative process can lead to poor substantive solutions, and yet offer the participants the opportunity to know each other and generate some solidarity among them. Or it can happen that a process produces good substantive solutions, but once concluded the participants lose all contact among themselves and no relational good is produced.

The relevance of each of these outcomes should also be evaluated on the basis of the nature of the task in hand, and of the degree of uncertainty associated with it. In practice, in a stable context, to take responsibility for a public good the conditions for production and use of which are entirely predictable, devolution pure and simple will be enough. Instrumental logic takes over, and can even go as far as reducing the variety of partners involved by handing it over to one single "agency" (specialised in the production of the good in question) concentrating specialised sectoral resources (as is seen, for example, in the administrations used for local public transport or its concession to specialised businesses). But, as soon as the problem becomes more complex, requiring the mobilisation of different competences and/or where sometimes the precise objectives are difficult to translate, mixed partnerships should be favoured. The emergence of relationships of trust between these actors, as well as their capacity to effectively manage the problems that arise, become in this more uncertain context objectives in their own right. Par excellence, questions of economic development fall into this category.

In the short run the instrumental outcomes are more relevant. The evaluator should estimate whether such results have been reached in an efficient way and whether they offer an appropriate response to the community problems. But in the long run policy makers should look especially at the relational aspects. The accumulation of social capital is a worthy mechanism, because it opens new possibilities for the future. So, in the long run, we should ask: what is left after the process has been concluded? What have the participants learnt? Were they able to reinforce their co-operation and to launch new initiatives, even when the incentives from central government were exhausted? The goal of regional policy is not only that of generating development, but also of generating local networks that will be able to design new solutions in the future.

The critical question of local capacity building

In all cases, one of the main challenges for the co-operation mechanisms described is to enhance the competence of local actors, a precondition for successful decentralisation. This applies not only to relationships between municipalities and access to knowledge through relations with private sector partners, but also to the sharing of skills which can result from relations with higher levels of government. In Korea (*OECD Territorial Reviews: Korea*), local governments are expected to effectively integrate sectoral measures provided by different ministries into a comprehensive policy for the development of their own jurisdiction. This requires broad knowledge and administrative skills, and reforms in the training of local public officials. For the time being in Korea, regional, provincial and metropolitan city governments have their own separate training institutes for local officials. Opportunities for local government officials to learn from central government officials or other local governments remain very limited so far, and intergovernmental exchanges of personnel could be encouraged, both vertically and horizontally. Personnel secondment is one possible method of learning, and could be further explored. For its part, Finland rests on the increasing use of co-operative practices and on the quest for coherence between mechanisms in the programme for the new regional development policy. It has also stressed the need to involve the different stakeholders not only in the implementation, but especially in the actual preparation of strategies, since this can only help motivate the actors involved (see OECD TDPC Symposium 2004).

Public authorities' competences have undergone change. In administrative tradition, the first duty of the civil servant is to conform: to established rules, and to orders received. In the framework of multi-level governance, "the question of conformity gives way to the question of relevance" (Calame, 2003). Where it is possible to invent the best-adapted responses locally by applying the guiding principles recognised by everyone, the actors will be held responsible if they fail to try to find such an adaptation. This "capacity for invention" and recognition of the competences of partners forms part of the responsibilities of the local authorities. One of the main ways in which central government can thus support local communities is to reinforce their capacity to act. Making them responsible is thus the primary way of strengthening their competences.

Relying on local competences is as much about the need for effective decentralisation as it is an objective in itself. The advantage of training the actors involved in the processes of governance is thus borne out by a certain number of mechanisms designed to spread, train and even persuade the local actors. It consists of standardising their knowledge, where that is possible, sharing experiences, including those at national level, following repetitive procedures, the monitoring of which will rely on incremental changes and the progressive readjustment of objectives, and finally using management charts and any other current management tools. These goals can be seen at work in the setting up of assistance agreements, the creation of observer functions, or in making available central government officials to local governments.[28]

Although practical and functional training is provided, qualitative training (i.e., creative thinking, brainstorming practices, teamwork spirit, etc.) remains marginal and could be significantly reinforced. Reforming the overall mentality of local public administration towards a more open and innovative system is a long-term task. In this respect, the private sector could perhaps offer a source of inspiration in terms of entrepreneurial culture. Some OECD countries have actually started to introduce new learning initiatives for their local public officials so as to generate know-how spillovers from the private sector and learn certain management skills (see Box 2.15).

Further along, it should be possible to set up common training efforts for the different categories of civil and public servants. This is where a common culture could be forged, even if later on division into various specialisations could be helpful. But one challenge remains: that of evaluating civil and public servants. Finally, one way to help local public officials develop their capacity to perform new responsibilities would be to set up precise self-evaluation criteria. Designing a set of accurate performance objectives and measurement standards would provide local public officials with useful guidance by giving them a clear idea of what is expected from them. In some cases, local governments can even be associated directly in the process of designing such criteria. In Spain for example, the Spanish Federation of Communes and Provinces (FEMP), the Observatory for the Quality of Public Services (*Observatorio de la Calidad de los Servicios Públicos*, OCSP) and the Ministry of Public Administration have involved local governments in the diffusion of self-evaluation tools, called EFQM (European Foundation for Quality Management) and CAF (Common Assessment Framework). The OCSP then ensures the training of local public officials to use those evaluation tools. In other countries, local capacity development came about through the establishment of new regional institutions. In Hungary, for example, with the first PHARE Regional Development Programme (*OECD Territorial Reviews: Hungary*, 2001), regional

> Box 2.15. **Example of learning initiatives for local public officials in OECD countries**
>
> The **US** is probably offering the widest range of private sector-led learning opportunities for civil servants. This trend has started quite early with the awareness that public managers would increasingly need a cross-understanding of public, private and non-profit organisations work. As a consequence, practices of "contracting out" have become a recurrent exercise. This is not only restricted to contracts with business or non-profit organisations, but governments also contract with other governments. Approximately 24% of local government services in the US are estimated to be delivered through contracting out. Between 1992 and 1997, around 96% of local governments contracted out a new service (Wagner and Hefetz, 2001).
>
> Also in **Germany** where the fundamental source of public officials' training used to be the federal, regional training institutes, the 1990s saw a remarkable evolution towards a more open and interconnected system. Local authorities started to request management courses and an increasing number of private institutions have responded to that demand. More active exchanges between public and private institutions have been fostered. For example, general polytechnics (*Fachhochschulen*) have created several public management courses mainly within their departments of business administration. Moreover, universities that had largely ignored the public sector have created master programmes in public management, such as the University of Konstanz and the University of Potsdam.
>
> In **Busan**, a new partnership programme started in 2003 so as to develop collaboration with the private sector. Some civil servants take a one-week internship in a large private firm in order to learn management techniques. Such learning possibilities should be more fully developed and encouraged (TR Busan).

development agencies were established on an experimental basis. These RDAs then played a key role in launching a pilot planning programme for the South Great Plain and South Transdanubia.

The difficulty and inadequacy of evaluation

Whether in regard to relations between municipalities, relations between the public and private sectors or vertical relations between levels of government, enough time must be allowed to establish shared references, a common "language" and a minimum degree of trust in the undertakings of the different parties. This makes it very difficult to evaluate how these mechanisms are working. But it makes it possible to fashion tools and construct co-operation networks that may prove to be effective in the long term for the programming and implementation of development strategies.

It is clear that such mechanisms suffer from a lack of tried and tested evaluation tools and even of appropriate performance criteria. This is due to the length of time needed to establish partnerships. It is also a result of the twofold objective which such institutional arrangements must pursue: that of the effectiveness of the tasks to be accomplished on the one hand, and that of effective co-operation in terms of the networks set up, on the other.

Whatever would be the results of the evaluation they can help to re-organise the operational aspects of the device but not to renounce to the share of responsibilities among levels of government. Commitments entered into concerning decentralisation (in countries that have taken this path recently or longer ago) seem today to be more or less irreversible. It seems to be a matter of political sensitivity to consider now that situations of increased autonomy do not amount to lock ins. Some solutions, that might be effective from an economic standpoint, are not from a sociopolitical point of view, as is illustrated by the case of mergers between municipalities. The implication of citizens in local democracy and their participation in the process of decision-making should not be considered as reversible, but constitute an objective "in itself" for creating new forms of governance.

The process of evaluation gains to be built in reference to "best practice" solutions. They are often the result of policies in favour of institutional experiments.

Governance is not a science. It is necessary to provide the stimulus for innovation and observation in order to find out what are good practices, because no satisfactory theory exists that determines the optimal choice. Governance thus looks to solutions that are satisfactory rather than seeking to identify solutions that are optimal. In practice, when the models do not allow optimal solutions to be found, how does one obtain information on the possible solutions? Experimentation, which allows training through practice, provides the answer to this question. Where there is imperfect information, with learning-by-doing, there are potential gains from experimenting with a variety of policies for addressing social and economic problems. For Oates (1999; p. 1132) it is also possible to defend the idea that federal states are especially well adapted for promoting "technical progress" in public policy because their institutional structure allows them more room for manoeuvre in their local choices. In the United States, a group of measures concerning social and environmental policy have in this way been initiated at the regional or local level before being adopted either by other public authorities, or even at the federal level. "States, of course, may learn from others that the diffusion of successful policy innovations may be horizontal as well as vertical". (Oates,

1999; p. 1133) Some have even noticed cumulative forms of diffusion of these innovations, strongly reminiscent of the S-curve of technological innovations (even though the examples are more often to do with "horizontal" diffusions – among the same levels of government – rather than "vertical" ones – across levels of government). Within the European Union today there exists a sort of reciprocal training that transcends the level of individual states. Experiences of strengthening regional and local democracy (or other forms of objective) within a State can serve the needs of others facing the same challenges (Delcamp and Loughlin, 2002).

Central action and experimentation: this dimension is important for regional competitiveness. In practice, information travels relatively fast regarding innovations that are put in place; but information about their value takes longer, especially for those who have had to set them up and invest in order to generate knowledge. This could act as a disincentive for those regions more interested in a "free ride", which will want to wait for information to emerge about the value of these innovative mechanisms before adopting them, without taking the risk of initiating them (and letting competing regions know). Central action that supports institutional innovation is therefore indispensable in order to correct the disincentive effects of going ahead without support (particularly through the practices of matching, in which central government shares the costs and the risks of new programmes put in place locally). Besides constituting a correction to the lack of incentives, this type of central support can bring coherence at the national level, choosing innovations that do not contain too many negative externalities for other regions, but also because, by being informed in this way from the beginning and throughout the process, the State can make early choices as to the initiatives to put in place in other territories.[29] In France, for instance, experimentation is today enshrined in constitutional law. The "right to experiment" for central government as well as local communities was upheld during the first wave of recent decentralisation reforms in 2003.[30] Parliament remains the guarantor of this process, authorising it upstream and evaluating it downstream. In Finland more autonomy at regional level and reinforcement of inter municipal co-operation are tested in some specific areas. These various institutional experiments are tools for progress in governance.

Notes

1. Which are considered to be the relevant categories for composite competitive capacity measures of territories (Weiler, 2004).
2. OECD High Level Meeting, "Innovation and Effectiveness in Territorial Development Policy", Martigny, Switzerland, 25-26 June 2003.

3. Or depending on the amount of local resources the local authority has been able to generate.

4. In federal countries, the budget available for sharing is sometimes determined by a mechanism known as "revenue-sharing" whereby the "rich" states contribute to the budget of "poor" ones. For example, public finance indicators suggest that Denmark and Sweden – recognised as unitary countries – are more "decentralised" than federal Germany, Mexico or the United States. Devolution in Great Britain, which occurred after 2000, is not yet reflected in those statistics.

5. Incentives theory analyses situations in which contracts are signed between a principal and an agent under imperfect and asymmetric conditions of information. In such cases, one of the parties to the contract – the agent – is in possession of relevant information that the other party – the principal – is not aware of. A moral hazard situation occurs when the principal is not in a position to observe the agent's decisions and actions. It is therefore desirable that the contractual arrangement include incentives to ensure that the actions of the agent really do target the agreed objectives and/or the disclosure of private information (FARES, 2002).

6. However, this does not mean that the institutional and legal framework does not matter. For instance, they do not exist in the United Kingdom, where similar problems of co-ordination existed that could have favoured their use, even though central government has created and strengthened the Government Offices in the Regions (GOs), which are committed to supporting the implementation of its policies through local government. The City Challenge, which later became the Single Regeneration Programmes, as well as the current programmes are based on tenders and the selection of projects submitted by local authorities, usually in partnership with private actors. Whereas a contract is required for the partnership, there is no contract between the central government and the applicant local authority. The reason is probably to be found in the fact that British local authorities are in law the creatures of Parliament, and the unitary conception of the contract in common law does not allow a contract to be entered into between the Crown and a local authority. However, the broad array of responsibilities devolved to the Scottish Parliament, the Northern Ireland Assembly and the Welsh National Assembly (which is not a parliament but a local authority, with no legislative powers) made it necessary to reconcile regional autonomy with the unity of the UK. This gave rise in 2000 and 2001 to new forms of agreements that are not legally enforceable contracts.

7. This is, for example, the case in some Italian contractual arrangements and in the ROM contracts in the Netherlands. Private local actors (businesses and associations) are also represented in the CESR (Regional Economic and Social Councils) that issue opinions and offer proposals to the French *conseils régionaux* under the planning contracts between the State and the regions.

8. This objective played an important role in Italy at the time of the adoption of law No. 142/1990 and is considered a positive consequence of the French state-region planning contract.

9. In France, no third-party complaints of failure to comply with "plan contracts" appear to have resulted in penalties. So the conception in France is a very restrictive one which sees contracts more as protocols of reciprocal agreements than as real legal commitments. The Swiss view is different, making the granting of funds for a number of years conditional on achieving the stated intermediary objectives (especially as regards spending controls).

10. Verwaltungsvereinbarung: this agreement is based on article 104a of the Basic Law; the agreement has 16 articles and 32 pages, and is completed by a protocol on the interpretation of a number of provisions on request of certain governments.

11. This objective was clearly stated by the former French Minister of Planning in 1982, when planning contracts between the State and the regions were first launched. Presenting the economic planning reform bill to parliament, Michel Rocard explained that planning without decentralisation could lead to "totalitarianism", whereas "decentralisation without planning could cause chaos". This objective can also be found in presidential decree No. 677/1976 in Italy, as well as in Spain.

12. For instance, France has a highly fragmented local government system, (the system became more fragmented after the reforms leading to decentralisation in the early 1980s) and local autonomy is protected by the constitution. France also relies heavily on administrative law. Public administrations frequently use administrative contracts to carry out their duties or to cover their needs. With the decline in legitimacy of centralised administration and "government by command" since the late 1960s, contracts appeared to be an alternative solution to keep institutional relationships working within the public sector. While planning contracts between the State and the regions may be the best known example, they are not, by any means, the only contractual arrangements across levels of government in the French context. On the contrary, contracts soon became the standard instrument the law provided, used even by departments for their own sectoral policies whenever responsibilities had to be shared, with local authorities being given competence while central government kept its responsibility for policy-making.

13. To avoid "moral hazard risks", long periods of consultation, preparation and negotiation are necessary before a contract can be drawn up. In France, the "upstream" phase took two years for the preparation of the present round of planning contracts between the State and the regions (*Contrats de Plan État Régions*) (from 1998 to 2000 for 7-year contracts from 2000 to 2006). In Italy, contractual procedures involve stringent selection between projects in order to secure funding.

14. The closest body to a co-ordinating body for territorial policy is the National and Regional Planning Bureau which has developed a new perspective of territorial/regional policy and provided a network for local authorities as well as other local actors. However, substantial integration of these measures and effective policy implementation has yet to be seen due to persistent compartmentalism.

15. Since January 2003.

16. This was put to the test in Switzerland, for example, where although public expenditure was not reduced by inter-municipal co-operation, it was found that the more Swiss communes co-operated with each other, the more they tended to extend the scope of their co-operation (Steiner, 2003).

17. The LEADER (Liaison Entre Actions de Développement de l'Économie Rurale) programme is a European Union programme for rural areas that has played a pioneering role. By promoting local development initiatives, managed and designed by groups of local representatives, it has had a major impact in creating synergies between rural businesses in the areas concerned. Many countries have adopted this approach at national level.

18. There are also more "defensive than offensive" forms of co-operation among municipalities. In this context, voluntary mutual adjustment policies between local, and sometimes regional, players mean that co-operation also, at times, acts as a defence against the introduction of more demanding arrangements such as

the setting up of regional and metropolitan agencies or councils, or the merger of local municipalities.

19. A representative case is the IRD Duhallow, a rural development company established in 1989, operating a LEADER and Mainstream Rural Development Programme in an area between the North West of County Cork and the East of County Kerry (about 1 880 km^2, population of over 30 000). It manages a staff of more than 16 qualified professionals in programmes that range from social inclusion initiatives, tourism infrastructure development, and cultural activities. Local authorities have a relatively small representation on the Board (two out of 25 members) (IRD Duhallow, *Annual Report*, 2002-2003).

20. Dafflon and Ruegg (2002) in their analysis of the case of Switzerland note that "this form of collaboration, which is supposed to resolve the discrepancy between institutional and functional territories, tends to cause as many problems as it solves".

21. While national power is centred in the town hall, the communities control the finances. Thus, the budget of the French city of Lille amounts to a little less than EUR 300 million, in contrast to EUR 1.3 billion for Lille's urban community (CUDL).

22. Even if sharing local taxes could be perceived as renouncing independence in countries where municipal autonomy is a building block of the national institutions (for example in Finland).

23. For example, the INTERREG programme distinguishes between "low", "intermediate" and "high" levels of integration, defined as: Low, if the border regions operate as separate socio-economic units (necessitating in the case of previous INTERREG programmes separate sub-programmes for each side of the border); Intermediate, if various forms of co-operation between public administrations, private business, and other interests from either side of the border exist (with partly integrated or closely co-ordinated management of INTERREG programmes); High, if the two sides of the border effectively function as a single socio-economic unit (in EU terms, this would mean cross-border institutions and a fully integrated management structure for programming). See European Commission (DG REGIO) (2000) for more information.

24. These may include common infrastructures, facilitating educational exchange, tourism activities, environmental protection, and maintaining water resources, parks and natural reserves, as well as other local facilities and their cross-border use, where projects have flourished.

25. For a more extended analysis of the scope and limits of horizontal collaboration, see *Territorial Review of Switzerland* (OECD, 2002).

26. "As opposed to a wider notion of governance, which consists of all conceivable notions of government, a stricter notion of governance implies that private actors are involved in decision making in order to provide common goods and nonhierarchical means of guidance are employed. Government by contrast indicates that only public actors are involved and the hierarchical steering can be used. Where there is governance private actors may be independently engaged in self-regulation, or a regulatory task may have been delegated to them by a public authority, or they may be regulating jointly with a public actor. This interaction may occur across levels (vertically) or across arenas (horizontally)" (A. Héritier, 2002).

27. For instance, the institutionalised PPP model involves the establishment of an entity held jointly by the public partner and the private partner. The joint entity

thus has the task of ensuring the delivery of a work or service for the benefit of the public. In the member countries, public authorities sometimes have recourse to such structures, in particular to administer public services at local level, for example, water supply services, waste collection services and the development of accommodation in districts in crisis. The legal aspect of the joint entity allows the public partner, through its participation as one of the shareholders and in the decision-making bodies, to retain a relatively high degree of control over the development of the projects, which it can adapt over time depending on the circumstances. It also allows the public partner to build up its own experience of running the service in question, while being able to call upon the support of a private partner. An institutionalised PPP can be set up either by creating an entity held jointly by the public sector and the private sector, or by the private sector taking control of an existing public undertaking.

28. Moreover, elected officials are often reluctant to sign themselves up, although they do not hesitate to encourage their partners to join training programmes. The fact that they have been elected validates their level of skill and discourages them from joining the programmes (Calame, 2003).

29. While this support for experimentation is backed by block grants, which are unconditional, it can still fail in its mission when there is not enough sharing of information with the central powers. By contrast, where central government is an attentive partner, giving conditional support to the project (depending on its cost and its expected impact, tying the stages of financing to the stages of project completion, putting in place bonuses for good performance), financial transfers will undoubtedly be more effective. This is worth considering in the sense that where the local authorities have no room to manœuvre at the outset, particularly where transfers are unconditional, all forms of innovation risk being stifled.

30. Some authors note, nonetheless, that the very notion of "the right to experimentation" reveals the exceptional freedom left to local initiative (Calame, 2003).

ISBN 92-64-00946-9
Building Competitive Regions
Strategies and Governance
© OECD 2005

Bibliography

Arndt, M., T. Gawron and P. Jähnke (2000), "Regional Policy through Co-operation: From Urban Forum to Urban Network", *Urban Studies*, Vol. 37, No. 11, p. 1903-1923.

Ashcroft, B. (2002), "The Scottish Economy" in N. Hood, J. Peat, E. Peters and S. Young (Eds.) *Scotland in a Global Economy: The 20:20 Vision*, Palgrave Macmillan, Hampshire.

Bachtler, J. (2001), *Where is Regional Policy Going? A New Paradigm of Regional Policy*, Report to EoRPA Regional Policy Research Consortium, European Policies Research Centre, University of Strathclyde, Glasgow.

Bachtler, J. and P. Raines (2002), *A New Paradigm of Regional Policy? Reviewing Trends in Regional Policy in Europe*, Report to EoRPA Regional Policy Research Consortium, European Policies Research Centre, University of Strathclyde, Glasgow.

Benneworth, P., M. Danson, , P. Raines and G. Whittam (2003), "Confusing Clusters? Making Sense of the Cluster Approach in Theory and Practice", *European Planning Studies*, Vol. 11(5), pp. 511-520.

Berman, D. R. (2003), *Local Governments and the States: Autonomy, Politics, and Policy*, New York, M.E. Sharpe.

Best, M. (2000), "Silicon Valley and the Resurgence of Route 128: Systems Integration and Regional Innovation", in J. Dunning (Ed.) *Regions, Globalization, and the Knowledge-Based Economy*, Oxford University Press, Oxford.

Bobbio, L. (2003), "Building Social Capital through Democratic Deliberation: the Rise of Deliberative Arenas", in *Social Epistemology*, Vol. 17, No. 4, pp. 343-357.

Calame P. (2003), *La démocratie en miettes : Pour une révolution de la gouvernance*, Éditions Descartes and Cie, Paris.

Charles, D., B. Perry, and P. Benneworth (2004), *Towards a Multi-level Science Policy: Regional Science Policy in a European Context*, Regional Studies Association, Seaford.

Coase, R. (1974), "The Lighthouse in Economics", *Journal of Law and Economics*, 17 (Oct.) pp 357-76

Collin, J-P. and J. Léveillée, with the collaboration of M. Rivard and M. Robertson, (2004), *Municipal Organisation in Canada: Tradition and Transformation, Varying from Province to Province*, Villes Régions Monde/Institut de Ciences Politiques i Socials/Centre per a la Innovacio Local, 50 p. (forthcoming).

Cooke, P. (2004a), "Regional knowledge capabilities, embeddedness of firms and industry organisation: bioscience megacentres and economic geography", *European Planning Studies*, Vol. 12, pp. 625-641.

Cooke, P. (2004b), *University Research and Regional Development*, Report to EC-DG Research, European Commission, Brussels.

Cooke, P. (2004c), "Regional Transformation and Regional Disequilibrium: New Knowledge Economies and their Discontents," in G. Fuchs and P. Shapira. *Rethinking Regional Innovation and Change: Path Dependency or Regional Breakthrough?* Kluwer.

BIBLIOGRAPHY

Cooke, P., M. Heidenreich and H-J. Braczyk (2004d), *Regional Systems of Innovation: The Role of Governance in a Globalized World* (Second Edition), Routledge, London.

Cooke, P. (2001) "Regional Innovation Systems, Clusters and the Knowledge Economy", *Industrial and Corporate Change*, Vol. 10, No. 4, pp. 945-974.

Cooke, P. and K. Morgan (1991), *Industry, Training and Technology Transfer: The Baden-Wurttemberg System in Perspective*, Regional Industrial Research Report No. 6, Department of City and Regional Planning, University of Wales College of Cardiff.

Crouch, C., P. Le Galès, C. Trigilia and H. Voelzkow (2001), *Local Production Systems in Europe: Rise or Demise*, Oxford University Press, Oxford.

Dafflon, B. and R. Jean (2002), "Innovations institutionnelle et logique 'de bas-en-haut' en Suisse", *Organisations et territoire, Réflexion sur la gestion, l'innovation et l'entrepreneurship*. Vol. 11, No. 2, p. 127-137.

DATAR (2002), *Les Contrats de Plan État-Région*, série Territoires en mouvement, La documentation française.

Dankbaar, T. (2004), "Embeddedness, Context, Proximity and Control", *European Planning Studies*, Vol. 12, pp. 691-701.

Delcamp A. and J. Loughlin (eds) (2002), *La décentralisation dans les États de l'Union européenne*, La documentation française, Paris.

Doloreux, D. (2004), "Regional Innovation Systems in Canada: A Comparative Study", *Regional Studies*, Vol. 38, pp. 481-494.

Dunning, J. (1992), "The Competitive Advantage of Countries and the Activities of Transnational Corporations", *Transnational Corporations*, Vol. 1.1.

DTI (2004), *Competing in the Global Economy: The Innovation Challenge*, DTI Economics Paper No. 7, Department for Trade and Industry, London.

DTI/DfEE (2001), *Opportunity for All in a World of Change*, Department for Trade and Industry and Department for Education and Employment, London.

Fares, M. (2002), "Canonical models of theories of contracts", in E. Brousseau and J.-M. Glachant (eds) *The Economics of Contracts*, Cambridge University Press.

Foster, K.A. (1997), *The Political Economy of Special-Purpose Government*, Washington, D.C., Georgetown University Press.

Garnsey E. and C. Longhi (2004), "High Technology Locations and Globalization: Converse Paths, Common Processes", *Int. J. Technology Management*, Vol. 28, Nos. 3/4.

Gaxie D. (1997), "Introduction : les chemins tortueux de l'intercommunalité", in Rémy Le Saout, dir., *L'intercommunalité. Logiques nationales et enjeux locaux*, Rennes, Presses de l'Université de Rennes, p. 11-21.

Garfoli, G and B. Musyck (2001), "Innovation Policies for SMEs in Europe: Towards an Interactive Model?", *Regional Studies*, Vol. 9, pp. 869-872.

Greffe, X. (2001), "Devolution of Training: A Neccesity for the Knowledge Economy", in *Devolution and Globalisation: Implications for Local Decision-Makers*, Organisation for Economic Co-operation and Development, Paris.

Haila, A. and P. Le Galès (2002), "Combining the maintenance of the welfare state and the competitiveness of Finland: The contradictions of urban governance in Helsinki" Paper presented at the Workshop "The politics of metropolitan governance", 30th ECPR Joint Sessions of Workshops, Turin, 22-27 March.

Hajer, M.A. and H. Wagenaar (eds) (2003), *Deliberative Policy Analysis; Understanding Governance in the Network Society*, Cambridge University Press.

Hassink, R. (2002), "Regional Innovation Support Systems", *European Planning Studies*, Vol. 10(2), pp. 153-164.

Hayashi, M. (2002a), "Congestion, Technical Returns and the Minimum Efficient Scales of Local Government Expenditures: The Case of Japanese Municipalities", Discussion Paper Series No. 01, Institute for Research in Business and Economics, Meiji Gakuin University, *www.meijigakuin.ac.jp/~hayashim/Works/optimalsizef/PDF*.

Hayashi, M. (2002b), "Incentives and Technical Inefficiencies in the Production of Local Public Services", Economic and Social Research Institute, Cabinet Office, Government of Japan, Tokyo.

Héritier A. ed. (2002), *Common Goods – Reinventing European and International Governance*, Lanham, Maryland, Rowman and Littlefield Publishers Inc.

Hilpert, U. (1992), *Regional Innovation and Decentralization: High Tech Industry and Government Policy*, London and New York, Routledge.

Huggins, R. (2004), *European Competitiveness Index 2004: Measuring the Performance and Capacity of Europe's Nations and Regions*, Robert Huggins Associates, Pontypridd.

Inman R.P. (1988), "Federal assistance and local services in the United States: The evolution of a new federalist fiscal order" in *Fiscal Federalism* Harvey Rosen (ed.) Chicago: U. Chicago Press pp. 33-74.

IRD Duhallow (2002), *Annual Report 2002/2003*.

Jehiel P. (1997) "Bargaining between benevolent jurisdictions or when delegation induces inefficiencies,"*Journal of Public Economics*, Elsevier, Vol. 65(1), pages 61-74.

Joumard I. and P.M. Kongsrud (2003), "Fiscal Relations across Government Levels", OECD Economic Department Working Paper No. 375.

Kanter, R. M. (1995), *World Class: Thriving Locally in a Global Economy*, Simon and Schuster, New York.

Keating, M. (1995), "Size, Efficiency and Democracy: Consolidation, Fragmentation and Public Choice", in Dennis Judge, Gerry Stoker and Harold Wolman (dir.), *Theories of Urban Politics*, London, Sage Publications, p. 117-134.

Krugman P. and A.J. Venables (1990) "Integration and the competitiveness of the peripheral industry", pp. 55-77 in Bliss, C. and J. Braga de Macedo (eds.), *Unity with Diversity in the European Economy*, Cambridge University Press/CEPR, Cambridge/London.

Lagendijk, A., and D. Charles, (undated) *Regional Institutions facilitating technology transfer to SMEs: A Review paper for OECD*, Organisation for Economic Co-operation and Development, Paris.

Landabaso. M., C. Oughton, and K. Morgan, (2003) "Learning Regions in Europe: Theory, Policy and Practice through the RIS Experience", in D. V. Gibson et al. (eds.) *Systems and Policies for the Global Learning Economy*, Praeger Press.

Lawton Smith, H. (2005), Invited keynote paper "The impact of tertiary education on urban development' OECD International conference on city competitiveness, Tenerife, March 3 and 4 2005.

Longhi, C. (1999), "Networks, collective learning and technology development in innovative high- technology regions: the case of Sophia Antipolis", *Regional Studies*, Vol. 33.4.

Longhi C. and M. Quere, 1997b, "The Sophia-Antipolis Project or the Uncertain Creation of an Innovative Milieu", in Ratti, Bramanti, Gordon (eds), *The Dynamics of Innovative Regions*, Eldershot, Ashgate Pub.

Lundvall, B.A. (1992) *National Systems of Innovation: Towards a theory of innovation and interactive learning*, Pinter, London.

Lundvall, B. A. and B. Johnson (1994), "The Learning Economy", *Journal of Industry Studies*, Vol. 1, pp. 23-42.

Luger, M.I. and H. A. Goldstein (1991), *Technology in the Garden*, Chapel Hill, N.C.: UNC Press.

Marcou, G. (2004), La planification à l'échelle des grands territoires. Etude comparative (Allemagne, Espagne, Italie, Pays-Bas, Royaume-Uni), Paris, Ministère de l'Equipement, du Logement et des Transports (forthcoming).

Marcou, G. and H. Wollman (eds.) (2004), Réforme de la décentralisation, réforme de l'État : régions et villes en Europe, CNRS éditions, Paris.

Markusen, A. (1996), "Sticky Places in slippery space: A typology of industrial districts", *Economic Geography*, Vol. 72. pp. 293-313.

Martin, R. and P. Sunley (1998), "Slow Convergence? The New Endogenous Growth Theory and Regional Development", *Regional Studies*, Vol. 74, pp. 201-227.

Martin R. and P. Sunley (2003), "Deconstructing Clusters: Chaotic Concept or Policy Panacea?", *Journal of Economic Geography*, 1, 5-35.

Martin, R. and P. Tyler (2000), "Regional Employment Evolutions in the European Union: A Preliminary Analysis", *Regional Studies*, Vol. 34, pp. 601-616.

Massey, D. and D. Wield (1992), "Evaluating Science Parks", *Local Economy*, Vol. 7, pp. 10-25.

Moiso A. and Uusitalo R. (2003), "Kuntien yhdistymisen vaikutukset kuntien menoihin", (The effects of amalgamations of municipalities on expenditure of municipalities). Sisäasiainministeriö, Finland.

Oates W.E. (1999), "An Essay on Fiscal Federalism" *Journal of Economic Literature*, Vol. 37, No. 3, Sept., pp. 1120-1149.

OECD (1997), *National Innovation Systems*, Organisation for Economic Co-operation and Development, Paris.

OECD (1999), *Report on Innovation and Territories: U-grading Knowledge and Diffusing Technology in a Regional Context*, Organisation for Economic Co-operation and Development, Paris.

OECD (2001a), *Territorial Review of Italy*, Organisation for Economic Co-operation and Development, Paris.

OECD (2001b), *OECD Territorial Outlook, 2001*, Organisation for Economic Co-operation and Development, Paris.

OECD (2001c), *Territorial Review of Hungary*, Organisation for Economic Co-operation and Development, Paris.

OECD (2002a), Benchmarking of Science Industry Relationships, Organisation for Economic Co-operation and Development, Paris.

OECD (2002b), *Territorial Review of Switzerland*, Organisation for Economic Co-operation and Development, Paris.

OECD (2002c), *Territorial Review of Canada*, Organisation for Economic Co-operation and Development, Paris.

OECD (2002d), *Territorial Review of Champagne-Ardennes, France*, Organisation for Economic Co-operation and Development, Paris.

OECD (2003a), *Territorial Review of Mexico*, Organisation for Economic Co-operation and Development, Paris.

OECD (2003b), *Territorial Review of Helsinki, Finland*, Organisation for Economic Co-operation and Development, Paris.

OECD (2003c), *Territorial Review of Öresund (Copenhagen and Malmo)*, Organisation for Economic Co-operation and Development, Paris.

OECD (2003d), *Territorial Review of Vienna – Bratislava*, Organisation for Economic Co-operation and Development, Paris.

OECD (2004), *Territorial Review of the Czech Republic*, Organisation for Economic Co-operation and Development, Paris.

OECD (2005), *Territorial Review of Japan*, Organisation for Economic Co-operation and Development, Paris.

OECD *Territorial Review of Finland*, Organisation for Economic Co-operation and Development, Paris, (forthcoming).

OECD (2004), *Territorial Review of Mexico City*, Organisation for Economic Co-operation and Development, Paris.

OECD (2004), *Territorial Review of Montreal, Canada*, Organisation for Economic Co-operation and Development, Paris.

OECD (2005), *Territorial Review of Busan – Korea*, Organisation for Economic Co-operation and Development, Paris.

OECD, *Territorial Review of Seoul – Korea*, Organisation for Economic Co-operation and Development, Paris. Forthcoming.

OECD (2002), *Territorial Review of Tzoumerka, Greece*, Organisation for Economic Co-operation and Development, Paris.

OECD (2003), *Territorial Review of Moravska Trebova-Jevicko, Czech Republic*, Organisation for Economic Co-operation and Development, Paris.

OECD (2000), *Territorial Review of Bergamo, Italy*, Organisation for Economic Co-operation and Development, Paris.

OECD (2001), *Territorial Review of the Valencian Central Districts, Spain*, Organisation for Economic Co-operation and Development, Paris.

OECD (2002), *Urban Renaissance Review: Glasgow: Lessons for Innovation and Implementation*, Organisation for Economic Co-operation and Development, Paris.

OECD (2000), *Urban Renaissance Review: Belfast*, Organisation for Economic Co-operation and Development, Paris.

OECD (2000), *Cultivating Rural Amenities: An Economic Development Perspective*, Organisation for Economic Co-operation and Development, Paris.

Patel, P. and Pavitt, K. (1991), "Larger firms in the production of the world's technology: An important case of 'non-globalization'", *Journal of International Business Studies*, Vol. 22, pp. 35-54.

Porter, M. (1990), *The Competitive Advantage of Nations*, The Free Press, New York.

Porter, M. (1994), "The Role of Location in Competition", *Journal of the Economics of Business*, Vol. 1, No. 1.

Porter, M. (2003), "The Economic Performance of Regions", *Regional Studies*, Vol. 37, pp. 549-578.

Power, D. and M. Lundmark, (2004), "Working through Knowledge Pools: Labour Market Dynamics, the Transference of Knowledge and Ideas, and Industrial Clusters", *Urban Studies*, Vol. 41, pp. 1025-1044.

Raines, P. (2001), "The Cluster Approach and the Dynamics of Regional Policymaking", September, EPRC Research Paper No. 47.

Reich, R. (1991), *The Work of Nations: Preparing Ourselves for 21st Century Capitalism*, New York: Alfred A. Knopf.

Rosenfeld, S. (1998), *Technical Colleges, Technology Deployment and Regional Development*, draft stock-taking paper prepared for the OECD, Regional Technology Strategies Inc, Chapel Hill, North Carolina.

Rosenfeld, S. (2002), *Creating smart systems: A guide to cluster strategies in less-favoured regions*, Regional Technology Strategies Inc, Chapel Hill, North Carolina.

Sancton, A. (2000), *Merger Mania: The Assault on Local Government*, Westmount, Price-Patterson Ltd.

Saxenian, A. (1994), *Regional Advantage: Culture and Competition in Silicon Valley and Route 128*, Harvard University Press, Cambridge, MA.

Scott, A. and M. Storper (2003), "Regions, Globalization and Development", *Regional Studies*, Vol. 37, pp. 579-593.

Simmie, J., J. Sennett, P. Wood and D. Hart (2002), "Innovation in Europe: A Tale of Networks, Knowledge and Trade in Five Cities", *Regional Studies*, Vol. 36, pp. 47-64.

Steiner, R. (2003), "The Causes, Spread and Effects on Inter-Municipal Co-operation and Municipal Mergers in Switzerland", *Public Management Review*, Vol. 5, No. 4, p. 551-571.

Storper, M. (1997) *The Regional World: Territorial Development in a Global Economy*, Guildford Press, New York.

Tornatzky, L., P. Waugaman, and D. Gray (2002), "Innovation U: New University Roles in a Knowledge Economy", Southern Growth Policies Board, Research Triangle Park, NC, *www.southern.org/pubs/innovationU/*.

Vermeylen P. (2001), "Public Private Partnerships and Urban Renewal", OGM preparatory report for the *Informal Councils of Ministers on Urban Policy*, Brussels.

Wishlade, F., Brown, R., and Yuill, D. (1996), *A Comparative Overview of Research and Development Incentive Policies in the EU*, Report to Ministry of Industry, France, European Policies Research Centre, University of Strathclyde, Glasgow.

Yuill, D. (2003), *Regional Policy in Europe, Annual Review, 2002/03*, Report to the EoRPA Regional Research Consortium, European Policies Research Centre, University of Strathclyde, Glasgow.

OECD PUBLICATIONS, 2, rue André-Pascal, 75775 PARIS CEDEX 16
PRINTED IN FRANCE
(04 2005 04 1 P) ISBN 92-64-00946-9 – No. 54049 2005